Rethinking Celebration

Other books by Cleophus J. LaRue
from Westminster John Knox Press

The Heart of Black Preaching

Power in the Pulpit: How America's Most Effective Black Preachers Prepare Their Sermons

More Power in the Pulpit: How America's Most Effective Black Preachers Prepare Their Sermons

This Is My Story: Testimonies and Sermons of Black Women in Ministry

I Believe I'll Testify: The Art of African American Preaching

Rethinking Celebration
From Rhetoric to Praise in African American Preaching

Cleophus J. LaRue

WESTMINSTER
JOHN KNOX PRESS
LOUISVILLE · KENTUCKY

© 2016 Cleophus J. LaRue

First edition
Published by Westminster John Knox Press
Louisville, Kentucky

16 17 18 19 20 21 22 23 24 25—10 9 8 7 6 5 4 3 2 1

All rights reserved. No part of this book may be reproduced or transmitted in any form or by any means, electronic or mechanical, including photocopying, recording, or by any information storage or retrieval system, without permission in writing from the publisher. For information, address Westminster John Knox Press, 100 Witherspoon Street, Louisville, Kentucky 40202-1396. Or contact us online at www.wjkbooks.com.

Sermon titled "Traveling toward the Sunrise," by Paschal Sampson Wilkinson Sr. is used by permission of the author's estate. Sermon titled "Rise: A Sermon," by Brian Blount, originally appeared in *Invasion of the Dead: Preaching Resurrection* (Louisville, KY: Westminster John Knox Press, 2014) and is used by permission of the publisher. Sermon titled "Tamar's Torn Robe," by Claudette Anderson Copeland, originally appeared in Cleophus J. LaRue, ed., *This Is My Story: Testimonies and Sermons of Black Women in Ministry* (Louisville, KY: Westminster John Knox Press, 2005) and is used by permission of the publisher. Sermon titled "It Will Surely Come," by Cleophus J. LaRue was previously published in the *Princeton Seminary Bulletin* 20, no. 2 (July 1999) and is used by permission.

Book design by Drew Stevens
Cover design by Marc Whitaker/MTWDesign.net

Library of Congress Cataloging-in-Publication Data

Names: LaRue, Cleophus James, 1953– author.
Title: Rethinking celebration : From Rhetoric to Praise in African American Preaching / Cleophus J. LaRue.
Description: First edition. | Louisville, Kentucky : Westminster John Knox Press, 2016. | Includes bibliographical references.
Identifiers: LCCN 2015051051 (print) | LCCN 2016016913 (ebook) |
 ISBN 9780664261498 (alk. paper) | ISBN 9781611646696 ()
Subjects: LCSH: African American preaching.
Classification: LCC BV4221 .L375 2016 (print) | LCC BV4221 (ebook) |
 DDC 251.0089/96073—dc23
LC record available at https://lccn.loc.gov/2015051051

∞ The paper used in this publication meets the minimum requirements
of the American National Standard for Information Sciences—
Permanence of Paper for Printed Library Materials, ANSI Z39.48-1992.

Most Westminster John Knox Press books are available at special quantity discounts when purchased in bulk by corporations, organizations, and special-interest groups. For more information, please e-mail SpecialSales@wjkbooks.com.

To Lori Ann

Contents

Introduction	ix
1. The Celebratory Impulse in African American Preaching	1
2. A Review of Henry Mitchell's and Frank Thomas's Celebration Homiletic	7
3. The Problem with Celebration as an Evocative Rhetorical Tool	19
4. Festivity Theory and the Origins of Celebration	31
5. A Theology of Praise in Its Multiple Expressions	47
Conclusion	69
Appendix: Sermons	73
Cleophus J. LaRue: "The Necessity of the Wilderness" (Mark 1:1–13)	73
Cleophus J. LaRue: "Why Bother?" (Acts 17:16–23)	75
Paschal Sampson Wilkinson Sr.: "Traveling toward the Sunrise" (Numbers 21:10–11)	79
Brian K. Blount: "Rise!" (Mark 5:21–24, 35–43)	83
Claudette Anderson Copeland: "Tamar's Torn Robe" (2 Samuel 13:1–20)	92
Cleophus J. LaRue: "It Will Surely Come" (Habakkuk 2:1–4)	98
Notes	103
Bibliography	117

Introduction

This book is a clarion call for African American preachers to think more deeply about the aims and ends of their preaching—namely, to stop putting so much emphasis on celebratory endings *to* our sermons and focus more on the substantive content *in* our sermons. Our so-called celebratory preaching, designed to excite the congregation into action through a highly emotional closing of the sermon, has had the opposite effect. Rather than inducing action, it has lulled generations of black congregants to sleep. While we are jumping up and down, shouting, and waving our hands in the air every Sunday during the worship hour, we seem not to notice the growing number of churched and unchurched alike who are becoming powerfully alienated from any form of institutional religion.[1] The rising category of the "nones"—Americans who are unaffiliated with brand-name religion—is on the rise in black churches as well as mainline congregations.[2] Our black communities are changing right before our eyes. They, like the rest of America, are becoming more secular, less knowledgeable about the Bible, and less spiritual.

In the face of this nationwide numerical decline in organized religion and amidst a growing biblical illiteracy, our emotional rejoicing in worship grows stronger and stronger while our understanding of Scripture and theology seems to grow weaker and weaker. We are emphasizing emotional rejoicing too much and substantive content in our sermons too little. Not only have we diluted the gospel through our lack of solid preparation for preaching, but all too many black preachers have privatized the faith, removed it from the public square, bought into some version of the prosperity gospel, and turned preaching into little more than motivational speech for the privatized longings of a consumer-oriented clientele.[3]

Even as I critique black preaching for its lack of prophetic witness, I am aware of the fact that there are untold numbers of black churches who continue to hold high the banner of prophetic witness even in the face of the many who have walked away. The prophetic preaching of the late Rev. Clementa Pinckney and the Charleston 9 is proof that all black ministers have not squandered the heritage passed on to them by Alexander Crummell, Francis Grimke, and others. But for every preacher like Charleston 9's Pinckney, who upheld the black tradition of preaching prophetic justice, there are a dozen black preachers who preach prosperity and flaunt their own lifestyle of conspicuous consumption

The church's traditional theological teachings are heard less and less in their traditional understandings, and what passes for good preaching is a mere echo chamber to the siren calls of our hedonistic culture with its endless appetite for material gain and self-advancement. The black church is unabashedly awash in the pursuit of material things and has been for some time.[4] And black preachers are leading the way. Thirty years ago Neal Postman in *Amusing Ourselves to Death* noted that television was making us "sillier by the minute":

> The decline of a print-based epistemology and the accompanying rise of a television-based epistemology has had grave consequences for public life, that we are getting sillier by the minute. . . . As typography moves to the periphery of our culture and television takes its place at the center, the seriousness, clarity, and above all, value of public discourse dangerously declines.[5]

No truer words were spoken as we witness the growing number of shameless black preachers joining the ranks of the reality TV crowd, displaying for the entire world to see the foibles and failures of black religious culture. The vulgarity and insipid tomfoolery exhibited by the reality TV preachers would put the *Amos 'n' Andy* sitcom of yesteryear to shame.[6]

In all too many pulpits, God has become little more than an "errand boy or girl" who gives us all we desire. Performance has replaced proclamation; in other words, more preachers focus on *how* they say something as opposed to *what* they say. Being known for having a "sweet whoop"[7] in one's preaching style is much preferred to having a sound message. So much that happens in black worship today is a form of emotional exercise that ultimately has little effect on what goes on in a person's life during the rest of the week.[8] In our YouTube age of instant entertainment, people also expect to be constantly entertained in matters religious. And all too many preachers are willing to oblige them in these opening years of the twenty-first century. Without a sound exegetical process and a theological tradition to guide us, ministers do "what [is] right in their own eyes" (Judg. 17:6). We preach as if we are no longer conscious of our surroundings and the great challenges before us.

Our black communities are stressed, and the people who populate them are, in many instances, broken and struggling to survive from day to day. Youth suicides are up; teenage pregnancies are an ongoing concern; high school dropout rates are disproportionately high; black-on-black homicides are through the roof; at least one-third of the black male population has had a negative encounter with law enforcement; and black net worth is sinking while debt is increasing.[9] Yet in all too many black churches our preaching does not even attempt to address these realities because we have aimed beyond the "hills of relevance" for all the wrong reasons. Like a laser beam, so much of our preaching today focuses, to the exclusion of all else, on that much ballyhooed celebratory ending. Our overemphasis on the manner in which we close out sermons and our burning desire to slay the crowd every Sunday have caused us to lose sight of the importance of the clear enunciation of the word of God in our preaching. The desire to navigate successfully that much sought-after celebratory, emotional high at the close of the black sermon is negatively affecting the ways in which preaching should strengthen the church and impact its wider witness to the world.

Black churches have traditionally pitched their tents where the needs were greatest, but today a great many of those tents, even when pitched in proximity to the black masses, no longer seem to house pulpits that speak *to* or *for* the black masses. Our ministers, young and old alike, seem more concerned with making a "rhetorical hit" in the pulpit than in preaching the unsearchable riches of Jesus Christ. I wish I could say that the black church of today would not be recognized by prophets on the order of Martin Luther King Jr., Samuel DeWitt Proctor, Gardner Taylor, Nannie Helen Burrows, and other great voices from our past, but the truth of the matter is that they would immediately recognize it, for it is the same church they railed against in their day for its lethargy and inertia. King made no effort to hide his contempt for black churches and black preachers who would not commit themselves to the movement for justice and equality:

> I'm sick and tired of seeing [black] preachers riding around in big cars and living in big houses and not concerned about the problems of the people who made it possible for them to get these things. . . . It seems that I can hear the almighty God say, 'Stop preaching your loud sermons and whooping your irrelevant mess in my face, for

your hands are full of tar. For the people that I sent you to serve are in need, and you are doing nothing but being concerned about yourselves.' Seems that I can hear God saying that it's time to rise up now and make it clear that the evils of the universe must be removed. And that God isn't going to do it by himself. The church that overlooks this is a dangerously irrelevant church.[10]

So many black churches today, even in their multifaceted forms and dimensions, are indeed bordering on being irrelevant. Princeton University professor Eddie Glaude pronounced the black church dead and no longer central to black life as a repository for the social and moral conscience of the nation. He chided the venerable institution for its lack of prophetic energy in a time of great need in black communities across America. According to Glaude,

> We have witnessed *the routinization of black prophetic witness*. Too often the prophetic energies of black churches are represented as something inherent to the institution, and we need only point to past deeds for evidence of this fact. Sentences like, "The black church has always stood for . . ." "The black church was our rock . . ." "Without the black church, we would have not. . . ." In each instance, a backward glance defines the content of the church's stance in the present—justifying its continued relevance and authorizing its voice. Its task, because it has become alienated from the moment in which it lives, is to make us venerate and conform to it.[11]

While I'm not prepared to declare the black church dead, I do believe that it is in the ecclesial intensive care unit and that its survival will depend, in part, on a revival of the quality of its proclamation on Sundays.

Black homileticians are also failing the church, for we have spent too much time talking about what is wrong with the preaching tradition of others and not enough time on how our knowledge of homiletics could be used to strengthen black preaching in our day. Some of our engagement with and critique of white homiletical theory has been necessary and helpful, for while there are some rudimentary skills that all preachers need to learn irrespective of race, class, or ethnicity, at some point, context does affect the form, content, and aims of our preaching. Consequently, blacks, like many other groups, have sought to participate in the nuancing that must take place when homiletical theory crosses into various contextual realities. For this reason black homileticians have rightly pointed out those places where white homileticians come up short in their theories about what makes for effective preaching. Given the lack of acknowledgment of black preaching's contribution to the homiletical enterprise, it is understandable that blacks would try to carve out an identity and name their unique contributions to the history of preaching over against the dominant stream of white homiletics. Such critiques benefit all parties concerned. What we gained in that period and through that literature of critique and challenge is an acknowledgment that there is a coherent, intellectually astute black homiletical tradition. But an endless engagement of contrasts and comparisons with white homiletics precludes the breaking of new ground in our own black tradition.

We cannot deepen our understanding of the particulars of black homiletical theory simply by contrasting and comparing ourselves to approaches to preaching espoused by those from another culture. What is obscured in such an exchange is the rich diversity within black religious circles. In our disagreement with white homileticians, we have failed to acknowledge the great diversity and nuancing that has always been a part of the black preaching tradition. *Rethinking Celebration* offers a corrective to current understandings of the celebratory impulse in black preaching and seeks to build on that earlier black homiletical literature as it relates to celebration in African American preaching and worship. Henry H. Mitchell, James Earl Massey, William McClain, James Forbes, and other black homileticians of their generation are to be commended for their work in advancing scholarship in African American religion, especially black preaching and worship. In *Rethinking Celebration* I seek to advance the argument by lifting to visibility some of the inner conversations and critiques within the black religious tradition.

Foremost among such conversations would be a new look at the importance and effectiveness of celebration in black preaching, long regarded as one of the most identifiable features of African American preaching. I will argue that effective preaching, by which I mean preaching that speaks powerfully to this present age while at the same time remaining true to sound scriptural/theological traditions, is being overshadowed by a misunderstanding of the place and theological significance of celebration. To suggest, as Henry Mitchell, Frank Thomas, and others have done, that the only way for African American congregants to remember and do something they've heard in a sermon is by engaging in some form of emotional rejoicing (celebration) at the close of the sermon strains credulity, and it tempts the preacher into placing too much firepower at the end of the sermon. Yet that is the gist of the celebratory argument being advanced by Mitchell and other pro-celebrationists. They maintain that if you want to convince black congregants to act on what they've heard in the sermon, you must get them up on their feet, clapping their hands and celebrating (i.e., engaging in emotional rejoicing) in worship. I will argue that the facts simply do not bear out their claim. We have the people up on their feet clapping and celebrating in our black churches, but when they are done with their celebration, there is very little to show in terms of redemptive acts of love, justice, and service to and for the world (*kosmos*) that God so loves (John 3:16). The binary quality of worshipful praise as adoration and action is often missing in our celebratory rituals. This has to change if we are going to speak in meaningful ways across the generational divides and to the many challenges facing black communities across America.

Chapter 1 outlines the development of celebration in the contemporary African American religious experience and the ways in which it has been understood to work most effectively in black sermon forms. Although the word *celebration* has a long history in the church's life, it has come to characterize what many believe to be a defining feature of African American preaching: a deliberately evoked, emotional rejoicing at the climax of the sermon. Henry Mitchell and Frank Thomas have been the major proponents of the development of this term in black homiletical circles in recent years. *Celebration* as defined by these two men has become the cornerstone of their homiletic. In chapter 2 I will review and critique Mitchell's and Thomas's works on celebration over the past forty years as well as their recently revised editions on the subject. In this review I will seek to show how their homiletic has been harmed by their quasi-theological definition of *celebration* and the misplaced importance they attach to evocative rhetoric.

Chapter 3 defines and describes the problematic understandings inherent in a merely rhetorical understanding of celebratory preaching. Mitchell's and Thomas's heavy rhetorical emphasis on celebration causes black preachers to work much harder than they should have to on the end of their sermons as opposed to the substantive beginning and middle of their sermons. This aiming for a celebratory close each Sunday often leaves many black preachers feeling crestfallen and dispirited if the sermon has not lived up to their expectations or received the kind of vocal affirmation from the congregation that they had hoped it would. Mitchell's and Thomas's misguided rhetorical emphasis on celebration overshadows its theological importance and relegates the word of God to an inferior status in much of black preaching where moralizing is often confused with proclamation. While exhortation (*paranaesis*) clearly has a place in Scripture, some blacks make it the be-all and end-all of their preaching, sensing that the exhortatory emphasis has great appeal among black congregants; an appeal that is more conducive to a celebratory close.

Chapter 4 outlines the origins of celebration in festivity theory and argues that what is happening in much of black preaching today is more akin to ancient understandings of festivity as revelry rather than the worshipful praise of God. The word *celebration* comes to us from historical understandings of festivity with an emphasis on exceptionality, excess, frivolity, and good times. However, according to some philosophers of virtue, it has always had a deeper spiritual meaning that ultimately points to the Creator God. Blacks are indeed having a *good time* in their worship and preaching experiences, but I contend that these emotional highs do not necessarily translate into praise. Having argued for a nuanced theological understanding of celebration as worshipful praise and not mere joy and revelry as defined by historical understandings of festivity, I will then address Mitchell's and Thomas's claims about the functional purposes of celebration: that emotional rejoicing helps us to remember and do what is heard in the sermon. Finally, chapter 4 addresses the bivalent nature of adoration and action as a way of demonstrating how the sermon works its way into praxis in other ways than the mere emotional rejoicing espoused by Mitchell and Thomas.

Chapter 5 outlines a theology of praise based on Scripture, offers a more nuanced definition of *doxology*, and suggests ways to enhance black preaching by introducing wider dimensions of praise that are equally legitimate in the preaching moment as well as in the congregational response to the preaching of the word of God. Having outlined different forms of doxological praise, I examine sermons from a representative sampling of American preaching styles that show how different types of doxological praise can be effectively incorporated into the sermon. I argue that true celebratory praise is not always determined by levels of excitement or exaggerated animation. I'm not arguing *against* celebratory praise, but I am arguing *for* the free flow of praise in its many and varied expressions and a proper understanding of its rightful place in the sermon. What I am opposed to is contrived rhetoric, purposely structured into our sermons in an effort to guarantee emotional rejoicing at the end—rejoicing that according to Mitchell and Thomas should help us to remember and do what we heard proclaimed in the sermon. Everything that has breath is instructed to praise the Lord, but that praise cannot be manufactured and must come from the depths of our hearts. Its manifestations are not always in the more demonstrative, exaggerated forms of praise that usually come to mind when we think of celebration.

1
The Celebratory Impulse in African American Preaching

Celebration is a term that has long been associated with the black religious experience in America. Ask someone to name an identifying feature of black worship, and more often than not some aspect of celebration will surface high on the list of defining characteristics. Many times the celebration being spoken of is associated with preaching. Thus it is often the case that when blacks and others use the word *celebrate* to describe black religious phenomena, they mean some form of celebratory response centered on the climactic close of the preaching of the sermon (this is especially true of those in the Free Church tradition). This way of viewing celebration is understandable given the number of recent books and essays that have been published with the words *celebration* and *preaching* in the title.[1]

Henry H. Mitchell, regarded by many as the dean of African American homileticians, has been the person most responsible for bringing the term *celebration* into the ecclesial and academic worldview of the black religious experience. With his publication of three books on black preaching from 1970–1990, he became the major proponent of celebration.[2] However, Mitchell was not the first to identify and examine the importance of this term in the worship experience of African American Protestants. With respect to nomenclature, *celebration* is not a term unique to black worship. The word has its roots in hundreds of years of liturgical tradition and cultural-festivity theory. Harvey Cox, professor emeritus of sociology at Harvard University, dealt with the term in the mid-1960s in *Feast of Fools*.³ In that work, Cox cited the African American worship experience as being typical of the type of celebration to which he was calling the American churches to return—a celebration that at its heart sought unabashedly to praise God and not merely to escape from reality:

> In observing the religion of the poor and the black in America it is clear that the ability to celebrate with real abandon is most often found among people who are no strangers to pain and oppression. All this suggests that real celebration, rather than a retreat from the reality of injustice and evil, occurs most authentically where these negative realities are recognized and tackled, not where they are avoided.⁴

Mitchell makes a passing reference to Cox's *Feasts of Fools* in his 1970 publication *Black Preaching*, and he outlines the various functions of celebration in his 1977 publication *The Recovery of Preaching*, but he does not make a concerted effort to flesh out a theory or theology of celebration until the publication of *Celebration and Experience in Preaching* in 1990.⁵ It was James Earl Massey, another notable African American homiletician, who engaged Cox more intentionally in the early 1970s. Massey, unpacking Cox's argument on the celebratory inclination of humankind in *Feast of Fools*, cited "festivity" and a "type of celebratory close" as defining characteristics of black preaching as early as 1974 in *The Responsible Pulpit*.⁶ Though Massey did not probe deeply into the importance of festivity in black culture and religion, he did make an effort to link African American celebration to affirmation and praise within the broader framework of festivity theory:

> Black preaching excels in being an invitation to joy, even in the midst of sorrow and struggle. It does so by means of strong affirmation about God and good and through the contagious note of witnessed faith. Whatever festivity and playfulness fill the black sermon are there because they have been *won* in the midst of sorrow and lament, making the sermon itself an open expression of faith that has worked its way through, and now speaks in praise of God.⁷

It was Mitchell, however, who wrote most extensively on celebration in the intervening years and is most often associated with its elaboration and modus operandi in black religion. Frank Thomas, a Mitchell protégé, followed on the heels of his mentor with the publication of *They Like to Never Quit Praisin' God*:

Following the thoughts of Henry H. Mitchell, I have long believed that the genius of African American preaching has been its ability to celebrate the gospel . . . Suffice it to say that celebration is the natural response when one has received and appropriated the assurance of grace of the gospel.[8]

In this work, Thomas sought to develop Mitchell's understanding of celebration more fully by constructing a specific pedagogy for how the concept of celebration was to be incorporated into sermons as well as how it was to be taught and used effectively in the liturgical life of black worshiping communities.

I will argue that after almost fifty years of African American scholars and others writing and reflecting on what it means to celebrate in black preaching, a corrective to the accepted wisdom regarding celebration is in order.[9] Not only will I offer a corrective specifically to Mitchell's and Thomas's understanding of what it means to celebrate in black preaching, but I will attempt to provide new ways for the black church to think more broadly and more creatively about what it means for preachers and congregants alike to engage in effective celebratory praise. While Mitchell and Thomas have added much to our understanding of how celebration happens, several theological and practical difficulties become evident when one tries to implement their celebration homiletic.

First, they have developed an affective (experiential) homiletic to which they have attached a cultural (festive) understanding of celebration, causing celebration to be understood primarily as a contrived rhetorical tool in the hands of a skillful preacher and responsive congregation as opposed to the spontaneous worshipful praise of God. Second, in the development of their homiletic, they have unwittingly detached celebration from its theological roots, where praise is more fittingly defined as a response to the experience of God's grace and power and to proclamation that bears witness to that experience.[10] One searches their homiletic in vain for a sound theological definition of *celebration* that holds up under the weight of the liturgical history of the term.

Third, Mitchell and Thomas have not only detached celebration from its theological roots as praise; they have assigned to it a pedagogical function (that which we use to teach congregants) that takes primacy over its theological importance as doxology (that which we first offer as praise to God). For them the importance of celebration is that it teaches us "to remember and to do" what we heard in the sermon, but beyond that it seems to have little significance in their homiletic. Their emphasis is on celebration as *function* and not on the intrinsic efficacy of the act itself as worshipful praise. This functional understanding of celebration, intended to evoke "emotional rejoicing" through the display of well-crafted rhetoric, causes their celebration to take a detour from efficacious praise to functional praise, thus skewing celebration from its primary aim—ritual acts of worshipful praise to God. I'm not arguing against Mitchell's and Thomas's teaching us how to celebrate—especially if that celebration expresses itself as praise and not simply emotional rejoicing. What I am arguing against is the prioritizing of a functional understanding of praise that stems from their contrived rhetoric.

Finally, the vacuum created by the loss of celebration as worshipful praise in their homiletic is instead filled with evocative rhetoric often masquerading as praise. Words purposely structured to evoke emotion take priority over the Word faithfully proclaimed, which leads to efficacious praise and also to the engendering of faith in the hearing of the people of God. Thus, by way of default, their misguided rhetorical emphasis, along with the importance they attach to evocative rhetoric for preaching, encourages the preacher to become an artful wordsmith though not necessarily a faithful expositor of the Word. When evocative rhetoric becomes the be-all and end-all of preaching, performance reigns supreme, worship becomes a show, a congregation becomes an audience, and the preacher becomes a star performer. Intentional or not, the end result is that in the implementation of Mitchell's and Thomas's homiletic, inspiration takes priority over proclamation! They have made celebration the midwife of the Word by implicitly claiming that it is through celebration that we come to faith.

Actually, it is through the hearing of the Word that we come to faith, and then we celebrate what we have heard, received, and been invited to participate in through our wondrous acts of praise for the great things God has done. It is the aim of preaching to bring others to the praise of God by way of what has been proclaimed in Scripture and sermon.[11] Praise in its deepest theological sense is the human response to God's glory, power, mercy, and love. It consists largely of an acknowledgment or confession of God's existence and grandeur, and it renders honor and glory to God.[12] The mere act of celebrating does not trigger our faith; rather, celebration erupts when we have heard and received the Word and rightly applied it to our hearts through the mediation of the Spirit! Celebration is not what we do in order to learn; it is what we do as a result of what we have learned: mainly, the recognition and embrace of God's gracious acts made known to us in the rightful exposition and reception of the Word.[13] Hear the psalmist in effusive praise declare, "Come and see what God has done . . . there we rejoiced in him" (Ps. 66:5–6).

Mitchell's and Thomas's primary emphasis should be on sound exposition in their homiletic, for faith comes through hearing—not through emotional rejoicing or ecstatic reinforcement: "So faith comes from what is heard, and what is heard comes through the word of Christ" (Rom. 10:17). We *remember* and *do* what we *hear* and *receive* in the word of Christ! Praise erupts, breaks forth even, from an effective exposition of the word—a word born through prayerful meditation and rigorous study and an undeterred asking after God, not concocted rhetoric contrived to evoke emotion. This love of evocative rhetoric, endorsed by Mitchell and Thomas, has been too inclined to push black preachers toward performance and away from sound and solid preaching. Augustine in the first homiletics text on record rightly noted that while all preachers should strive to be both eloquent and wise, if they could not be both, they should at least be wise. He maintained that those who speak eloquently are heard with pleasure while those who speak wisely are heard with profit.[14] Wisdom is sorely lacking in much black preaching today.

Also, Mitchell and Thomas have too narrowly defined celebration as word-centered revelry set apart from corporate worship and happening only at the end of the sermon; thus their emphasis is on an animated doxological denouement. There are a number of ways and places to effectively engage in the praise of God throughout the worship service that move us beyond the narrow confines of their word-centered emphasis. Robert Smith Jr., in *Doctrine That Dances*, has rightly noted that the doxological response in the preaching and hearing of the Word of God does not enter the sermon in its conclusion; rather, it begins the sermon in its introduction and resounds throughout the message.[15] Smith's broader understanding of celebratory praise, I believe, is the more expansive and enduring. A deeper understanding of celebration requires us to broaden our view to include much more than emotional rejoicing or climactic utterance that comes at the close of the sermon. True ritual praise in worship involves more than a climactic moment centered on preaching; to the contrary, it should involve not just a moment but a day of celebration set aside for the purpose of giving praise and thanksgiving to God. Psalm 118:24 says, "This is the *day* that the LORD has made; let us rejoice and be glad in it" (emphasis added). We don't simply celebrate for a moment at the conclusion of preaching; we celebrate the entire Lord's Day. Other moments and forms of celebration are equally fitting and equally legitimate in the ritual acts of worshipful praise that take place in the worship setting and beyond. We celebrate God the Father, Son, and Holy Spirit; we celebrate the font and the baptisms, the Word and the Eucharist, the songs and the prayers, the gifts and the anointings, the liturgy and the assembly. And we most assuredly celebrate in our dance before the Lord in spite of those who complain of the modern-day eroticization of the liturgy in the church's liturgical dancers.[16] It is the entire day and the full worship experience that we celebrate and give thanks to God. In the Old Testament, celebration was centered on a feast or festival, with eating, singing, and the playing of instruments.[17]

As important as the climactic celebration of the word of God is, it is not and should not be the only time blacks consider themselves to be celebrating in worship or the only time that celebration is understood to be happening. The animated histrionics and expressive vocal praise that take place in many black churches during the preaching of the gospel are not the only metrics for gauging effective praise. Although there may be special times to praise God, the whole of Christian existence should somehow be dedicated to it. God's wonders should be proclaimed and praised not only with the voice but with one's entire life.[18] Our understanding of praise must be broader than Mitchell's and Thomas's word-centered emotional rejoicing. It is my belief that Mitchell's and Thomas's homiletic, with its heavy emphasis on cultural celebration, is in desperate need of a theology of praise that will provide celebration with a theological grounding, situate it in its rightful place in the church's worship, and broaden its parameters regarding what constitutes legitimate praise.

2

A Review of Henry Mitchell's and Frank Thomas's Celebration Homiletic

A REVIEW OF MITCHELL'S *CELEBRATION AND EXPERIENCE IN PREACHING*

In *Celebration and Experience in Preaching*[1] Mitchell develops a homiletic on the basis of two major points: the importance of an experiential encounter in preaching and a celebratory close at the end of the sermon. With respect to the experiential, Mitchell notes that despite the clarity of the biblical position on recognizing the whole human at all times, Western culture had for centuries preached primarily to the mental faculties, emphasizing the appeal to reason to the virtual exclusion of other gifts. Mitchell argues that such detached, objective reasoning as faith was unthinkable to the Hebrew mind-set. He is convinced that contemporary homileticians have yet to target sermon preparation to feelings in any disciplined way. In fact, he believes there is still much to be learned about preaching that addresses the totality of humankind in a manner consistent with Jesus' affirmative and holistic summary of the First Commandment.[2]

Mitchell calls for a type of preaching that speaks to holistic goals, content, and methods that affect all sectors of human consciousness. These are prerequisite if one's efforts are to be used by the Holy Spirit to plant faith in the deepest and most complete sense. The faith assumed to be the goal of such preaching is also holistic, requiring the hearer to be involved wholly in the sermon event in order to beget or nourish a faith that involves the entire person.[3] The preacher's goal, according to Mitchell, is to move the hearer's supporting core beliefs and entire lifestyle closer and closer to the new person in Christ. While this kind of preaching will certainly include information and reasoning, its main goal is not to provide information but rather to reach the listeners in the depths of their beings where trust and distrust reside. Holistic preaching is intended to reach gut-level belief and not merely intellectual assent.[4] In Mitchell's homiletic, this priestly effort to propagate a holistic faith becomes the foundation for all other aspects of the Christian's life and work. Thus it is crucial to his understanding of effective preaching. Such a faith as this is not begotten by human reasoning or cognitive discipline. Mitchell believes that

> it resides in the intuitive region, that great, right-brain storehouse, whose content has not been entered into the human bank by rational criteria and processes. If one's faith has no emotive dimension and involvement, it is cold and without depth. . . . Sane faith must be born in a reasonable encounter, but it is not born of rational argument. Nor does it reside primarily in the spheres of the mind where logic is the dominant function.[5]

In Mitchell's homiletic, the faith on which people bet their lives comes *not* because one has heard and understood a great flow of logical persuasion, though the love of God demands that we understand all we can; rather, it is the fruit of holistic encounter with familiar images, whatever one's intelligence might be.[6]

Lest it appear that Mitchell has completely ruled out rational concerns and human reasoning, he quickly adds that every sermon must make sense; it must be manifestly reasonable and generally consistent with an orderly understanding of God's creation and our experience in it. But, says Mitchell, although reason clears the way or opens the gate to the intuitive, it does not itself beget faith:

> Therefore, when one has arrived at an acceptably cogent flow chart or outline of sermon ideas, one has only begun the preparation by ensuring that its very flow will not be an intellectual obstacle. The demanding task of giving birth to faith and nourishing it remains. One has yet to address the more operatively relevant realms of human personality, such as intuition and emotion.[7]

No amount of isolated or pure reason can cause belief to happen. Reason may make straight the highway or prepare the path, but faith invades our lives through the intuitive and emotive sectors of consciousness. Mitchell believes that the intuitive realm where faith invades our lives is affected more directly by experiential encounter. These experiential encounters are stored in what Mitchell calls "tapes":

> The "tapes" of intuition contain impressions gathered and stored during the flow of life. This input is not examined, adopted, or organized in a *consciously* rational manner. It includes a wide variety of insights from culture, family, church, school and community, and individual experience. . . . Intuition can be guilty of harboring prejudice, but it may also contain most if not all of our highest and most valid values and insights. Indeed, its wisdom is quite frequently superior to that of rational consciousness.[8]

Mitchell claims that we live out our lives from this data base, and since much of this storehouse is verifiably sound, he thinks preachers should show a greater concern about the intuitive process in order to help people to improve their intuitive tapes or habitual replays of responses to particular circumstances. Rational screening certifies only that it is safe to open the door to the room where the intuitive tapes are kept. One's principal locus of belief and unbelief is inside this deep chamber of intuition and beyond the direct reach of propositional communication or logical argument.[9] It is the intuitive channel of communication that is used by the Spirit in the begetting and nourishment of faith. That being the case, Mitchell then asks, What means of communication can reach the intuitive consciousness of a wide spectrum of intelligence quotients at the same time? His answer is experiential encounter!

The term *experiential encounter* is used here to denote a homiletical plan in which the aim is to offer direct or vicarious encounters with and experiences of truths already fully certified as biblical, coherent, and relevant. Based on this definition, a sermon for Mitchell is a reasonable and relevant sequence of biblical affirmations planted in or offered to the intuitive consciousness of hearers by what might be called "homiletical co-workers" with the Spirit. This work is done by means of an assortment of rhetorical vehicles, or literary genres, that stimulate the hearer to identify with and take part in these very meaningful experiences. One is helped personally or vicariously to enter the spiritual-theological dynamics of an encounter with the Godhead or a fellowship with biblical or other historical or current characters, and the miracle of faith takes place. The intuitive impact of experiential encounter is a very important part of the resources by which God moves to create the miracle of faith.

The second major component of Mitchell's homiletic, which is the focus of this book, involves an understanding of expressive celebration, described by Mitchell as another resource used by God in the miracle of faith. Mitchell defines this expressive celebration as "emotional rejoicing."[10] In defense of this kind of emotional rejoicing he says, "It is time to deal with the nurture of faith by means of warm and intentionally emotive sharing of the gospel, concluding with sound and spontaneous emotional expressions called 'celebration.'"[11] He chides those who resist this kind of rejoicing in the presence of God, believing that it should be understood as thoroughly biblical. As proof, he cites Deuteronomy 12:12: "And ye shall rejoice before the LORD your God." Noting that many of the most significant and moving passages in the Bible are characterized by praise and celebration, Mitchell says that few Christians are probably aware of just how unbiblical it is to be as solemn and stern as most worshipers in Western culture tend to be.[12]

Not only is this emotional rejoicing biblical, according to Mitchell, but it is also historical. In the history of the church, the traditional use of the word *celebration* in connection with the mass of the Roman Catholic Church is indicative of a historical association of worship with emotional rejoicing. He also notes that the Shorter Catechism of the Presbyterian churches plainly states that the chief end of humankind is to glorify and *enjoy* God forever. He argues that historical understandings of dualism and confusion between the words *emotion* and *emotionalism* are reasons for Western inhibitions against displays of emotion in worship. In order to remove those inhibitions, Mitchell believes preachers need to become more intentional about emotion in worship as a whole. Preaching, as the key element in Protestant worship, has been all along under the obligation to be warm, or emotionally moving, yet, says Mitchell, we have not faced squarely this emotional character inherent in preaching:

> The powerful effects of emotion must begin to be systematically utilized, rather than merely tolerated. This is mandated, if faith at the level of core belief and practice is to grow. Just as muscles must be exercised to develop physically, so must feelings. . . . Just as we have chosen moving hymns, so must we choose elements in preaching that exercise high emotions like faith, trust, love, and hope.[13]

Mitchell's call for an embrace of emotion in preaching and worship is not confined to African American worship and preaching. The act of celebrating is not simply a cultural distinction of a particular ethnic group. Says Mitchell, "It is universally true that people recall far better what they have celebrated well. And they are far more apt to grow in Christian behavior-areas about which they have authentically rejoiced." In a sign of things to come, Mitchell then quotes Frank A. Thomas, one of his DMin students at the time, who added, "'They [the people] will neither remember nor practice what they have not celebrated.'"[14] At this point, Mitchell defines celebration as getting emotional about something, or a way to ecstatically reinforce something:

> Celebration is therefore to be sought, among many other reasons, for the way in which it can lift up the "meat" of the message and render it unforgettable. . . . High commitment and deep trust are far more likely to develop in an emotionally charged atmosphere.[15]

Decrying any suggestion of anti-intellectualism in his call for unabashed displays of emotion in worship, Mitchell cites educational research to confirm his idea that what we celebrate (get emotional about) we retain far longer. Citing the dangers in not allowing for celebration during the preaching moment, Mitchell says,

> The ultimate price for failing to nurture authentic celebration is that joy inhibited in expression is joy diminished or outright lost. The manners in which it is expressed may vary greatly. . . . But genuine joy does not exist without some form of release or expression. . . . The tragic implications are either that the sermon without a celebration is without some portion of the Word worthy of such, or that the inhibition toward deserved celebration and rejoicing causes the material preached to lose its greatest possible effect with the total person.[16]

Under the chapter heading of "Sermon Celebration" Mitchell moves to describe in depth how the newfound acceptance of emotion is taken to its logical conclusion in the sermon's celebratory close.[17] He is convinced that celebration is the best way to motivate people to do the will of God.[18] Arguing against the idea of the preacher simply winding down and taking a seat at the conclusion of the sermon, Mitchell believes the preacher/performing artist should engage in a final, triumphant, or celebrative expression of the theme or the resolution of the conflict or issue raised in the sermon.[19] Why should sermons close in this manner? According to Mitchell, it is because people do what they celebrate. He adds, the surprising good news is that celebration is the best way to get people to do the will of God:

> Only *positive* truths about God through Christ give healing and empowerment, causing great rejoicing and praise. The more people rejoice about the goodness and faithfulness of God, the more they establish that joyous quality or atmosphere in the psychic space of their inner lives, regardless of outer chaos. . . . One is more apt to work for justice after celebration of the justice of God, or one's high place in God's plan, than to respond to a pointed rebuke. People are motivated more by love and joy than by fear or even by negatively "prophetic" utterance.[20]

In further defense of his call for emotional rejoicing at the end of the sermon, Mitchell argues that if the gospel is good news, there is a sense in which the sermon should be somewhat celebrative from the very start. There ought not to be an exclusively intellectual and solemn section, after which comes the second or happy part. It is just good theology to insist that the tone of the good news be joy and celebration.

In a subsection titled "Some Working Understandings concerning Emotion," Mitchell begins to describe the pedagogical function of celebration as he attempts to help the uninitiated preacher launch into "the strange new world of intentional emotive expression."[21] He first admonishes preachers to practice an irrevocable commitment to high purpose when it comes to the use of emotions. Second, Mitchell urges people to avoid a message unless they feel deeply about the subject. Says Mitchell, "If the preacher does not care greatly about the text and its meaning for the hearers, then why should they[]?" He adds, "The spoken word has power to move persons only to the extent that it has already moved the speaker." Intentional or not, Mitchell seems to be suggesting a canon within a canon by suggesting that preachers should only preach from scriptural texts that have the ability to move the hearers deeply.

Third, Mitchell calls for emotional considerations to be a part of sermon preparations from the very outset. Citing the inescapability of emotion, he wants preachers while at their study tables to weigh each homiletical move for impact or effect, making sure, so far as it is in their power, that the emotional impact and suspense ascend progressively to the final celebration—that is, to the final moment of expressive joy:

Just as a dramatist writes a play whose acts move up to the resolution of the conflict, and just as a composer creates a symphony whose movements climb to the last crescendo, a sermon lifts up and finally celebrates the Good News.[22]

In summary, Mitchell's homiletic is based on experiential encounter and expressive celebration (emotional rejoicing) as the best ways to get people to hear and heed the gospel. While he is not opposed to rational argument, he believes that the cognitive approach is not the only way, nor necessarily the best way, to engender faith; intuition and emotion are genuine paths to faith also. He then assigns celebration a pedagogical function by describing the different ways in which it can be employed in the sermon. He defends his functional use of celebration by saying that people remember and do what they celebrate.

A REVIEW OF FRANK THOMAS'S *THEY LIKE TO NEVER QUIT PRAISIN' GOD*

Mitchell protégé Frank Thomas, in his revised edition of *They Like to Never Quit Praisin' God*, seeks to develop more fully the homiletical theory behind Mitchell's work on celebration. Thomas moves celebration further into the arena of pedagogical function in his attempts to devise a theory and method for teaching preachers how to construct celebratory sermons. He begins to lay the groundwork for this theory of emotional process with his definition of African American preaching: "The nature and purpose of African American preaching is to help people *experience the assurance of grace* (the good news) that is the gospel of Jesus Christ."[23]

He names the preaching tradition that helps people to experience this assurance of grace "celebrative design" because he believes that "celebration is the natural response when one has received and appropriated the assurance of grace of the gospel."[24] Like Mitchell, Thomas believes that the genius of African American preaching has been its ability to celebrate the gospel.[25] He, too, argues against the deductive, rationalistic methodology taught in many homiletics classes by Euro-American homileticians. Thomas believes that sermons that are rationalistic in approach merely lead to logically deduced truth and intellectual assent, minus any heartfelt, experiential embrace.[26]

Thus, Thomas's thesis is that celebration, moving at the level of emotional process, is the most effective method and vehicle to assure that Christ's grace reaches peoples' core beliefs.[27] He then defines *celebration* as "the culmination of the sermonic design, where a moment is created in which the remembrance of a redemptive past and/or the conviction of a liberated future transforms the events immediately experienced."[28] Thomas's definition of *celebration* is confusing at this point because he is not providing a theological definition of the term but merely describing when celebration happens—that is, it happens (culminates) at the climactic point of sermonic design. He then proceeds to define "sermonic design" as

> an emotional process that culminates (climaxes) in a moment of celebration when the good news (the assurance of grace) intensifies in core belief until one has received an inner assurance, affirmation, courage, and feeling of empowerment. One experiences oneself as victorious (that is, saved, set free, healed, encouraged, and so on) regardless of the external tragic circumstances of life.[29]

Celebration and sermonic design are intertwined in Thomas's homiletic, and they feed on each other in a Catch-22 scenario: Celebration is the culmination of sermonic design, and sermonic design is an emotional process that culminates in a moment of celebration.

Thomas then describes his method for achieving celebrative design through the emotional process. He argues that if preachers want to move beyond the natural limits of the cerebral process and focus on the emotional context rather than the right words (i.e., the cognitive context), they should incorporate the following five functional elements into their sermons:

1. *Use of Dialogical Language:* The preacher who is concerned about emotional process must use language that fosters dialogue between the preacher and the people.
2. *Sermon Must Appeal to Core Belief:* Contained within the intuitive aspect of the self is the collection of core beliefs, broad principles for living shaped by cognitive, emotive, and intuitive evaluation of life experiences. Emotional process and context involve all three as equal partners in reaching core belief in the preaching process.
3. *Concern for Emotive Movement:* This functional element involves the direct intention to arouse emotion and move people. Celebrative design does not move people as an end in itself but rather as a part of the emotional process whereby the message of

the sermon shifts into the intuitive core belief of the hearer. In Western homiletics, movement of thought is primarily cognitive, but in celebrative design movement is experienced at the level of emotion.
4. *Unity of Form and Substance:* Substance is content, the sum total of truth to be delivered to the people. Form is rhetorical strategy, the means of persuading people of the truth. The two must merge into one when emotional process is taken seriously.
5. *Creative Use of Reversals:* The preacher must give careful attention to paradox, for reversals are fundamental to human life and to human communication.[30]

Thomas returns to a description of celebration in his chapter titled "Guidelines for Celebration." In this instance he defines *celebration* as "climactic utterance" and once again describes how it functions:

> Celebration in the final stage of the sermon functions as the joyful and ecstatic reinforcement of the truth already taught and delivered in the main body of the sermon. . . . Lifting up the good news of the sermon, the preacher joyfully and ecstatically celebrates it to reinforce meaning in core belief.[31]

He notes that celebrative emotions are a natural and inherent part of the gospel: "Whenever the gospel is received and personally appropriated in core belief, celebrative emotions such as praise and thanksgiving are part of the intuitive experience and response and these celebrative emotions usher in the transformative power of the gospel."[32] It is important to note that celebration for Thomas operates in a strictly functional capacity. It's not what celebration is that makes it important for his homiletic; it's what celebration does.

Having argued for an emotional process that guarantees celebration, Thomas outlines a content-preparation process that will yield a celebrative sermon. His guarantee of a celebrative sermon is based on three assumptions: First, in order to develop content for a sermon that celebrates, there must be an experientially oriented preparation process. Experiential orientation means that the sermon is prepared from the cognitive, emotive, and intuitive aspects of human awareness. Second, the preacher must place him- or herself within a framework to experience the sermon in preparation. If the goal of the celebrative sermon is for people to experience the assurance of grace and if the people are going to experience the sermon in delivery, then the preacher must experience the sermon in preparation. Third, sermons that order and shape experience only happen at the intersection of the streets of life and the biblical text; therefore, in the celebrative sermon, it does not matter which comes first: the biblical text or the sermonic idea. He then lists prayer, free association, homiletical exegesis, and a preaching worksheet as key ingredients to the preparation of the celebratory sermon.[33]

The preaching worksheet is made up of six sections, each containing a set of questions that are quite conventional in terms of the fundamentals of sermon preparation, with the exception of section 6: "Strategy for Celebration." Contained in this section are three questions:

> 6a. What shall we celebrate?
> 6b. How shall we celebrate our response to [the content of] 6a?
> 6c. What materials of celebration shall we use?

Section 6 is supposed to help the preacher intentionally and specifically plan to celebrate the good news in the sermon. He describes most of the questions on the worksheet as *what* questions, except when he gets to 6b which he states as a *how* question:

> Question 6b asks, *how* shall we celebrate the *what* of 6a? Practically and concretely, *how* will we structure the sermon so that the *what* of 6a (the content) is delivered at the right moment with the right sense of timing?[34]

The structure he suggests is in the intuitive form of situation-complication-resolution-celebration. He argues that the preacher manages the emotional process of the sermon by clearly and experientially setting forth the situation and complication, and when the good news is supplied to resolve the complication, the sermon moves up to celebration. Having supplied a structure for celebration in 6b, Thomas then moves on to 6c—the materials to be used in the celebration. There is nothing inherently celebratory about the materials for celebration. In fact, Thomas seems to suggest that it is not the material (content) itself that is celebratory but rather the manner in which it is presented: "Materials of celebration could be the use of stories, scripture, music, poems, and the like to joyfully and ecstatically reinforce the good news of the sermon."[35] Here again it is the lack of a theological definition of *celebration* that turns Thomas's celebratory moment into little more than emotional rejoicing.

A weak link in this homiletic, therefore, is that there is no sound theological definition for *celebration*. Thomas describes a function of celebration but not a definition of the term: "Celebration in the final stage of the sermon functions as the *joyful and ecstatic reinforcement of the truth already taught and delivered in the main body of the sermon.*"[36] For Thomas, celebration happens (culminates) when you remember a redemptive past or when you have the conviction of a bright future.[37] When celebration happens is a function of celebration, but the definition is emotional rejoicing. To wit, his definition of *celebration* could read, "Emotional rejoicing happens when one remembers a redemptive past or has the conviction of a hopeful future." To this end he lacks a theological definition and thus allows rhetoric and intensive feelings to carry the day.

3
The Problem with Celebration as an Evocative Rhetorical Tool

Whether intentional or not, Mitchell's and Thomas's homiletic encourages an understanding of celebration not as worshipful praise but as evocative rhetoric that results in festive revelry. By *evocative rhetoric* I mean crafted or spontaneous speech intended to evoke an emotional response in the listeners. Expressions of emotion, not enlightenment, are the aim of this rhetoric. In all too many black churches—amongst clergy and laity alike—celebration has come to be regarded as little more than a surefire rhetorical tool that one unleashes on the congregation at the climactic height of the sermon. This type of celebration seeks to evoke, if not outright ensure, an exuberant denouement to the preached word. Further, Mitchell and Thomas argue that this much-sought-after climactic close, intentionally structured to erupt into emotional rejoicing, is to be *used* by the preacher to help worshipers remember and do what has been proclaimed in the body of the sermon. Many blacks labor under this understanding of celebration not as praise but as evocative rhetoric designed to drum up a dramatic close (revelry) to the sermon.

The problems with this understanding of celebration aimed primarily at the emotions are many. First, it obfuscates the aim and purpose of the sermon. A primary aim of an effective sermon is not merely to solicit an emotional response—even one that's put to good use—but rather to explicate the Scriptures with such clarity and insight as to make a claim on individuals when they hear the word of God proclaimed. It is the claim—heard and received—that God's word makes on us that moves us from sedentary listeners to active participants. While an affective presentation may make that claim easier to embrace, there is no guarantee that a claim has been heard or accepted simply because of the presence of emotion in the preacher or the hearers.[1] Faith, defined as the positive response of the total person to the initiatives of almighty God, comes through what is heard in the preaching of the gospel—not through what is celebrated—and what is heard comes through the word of Christ (Rom. 10:17). Lest black preaching be thought of as mere mindless, emotive chatter, there has to be room for intellectual assent in the preaching and hearing of the gospel. Augustine was also of the belief that you nourished the soul through the feeding of the mind.[2]

While it is clear that Mitchell and Thomas believe that whites and other mainliners have gone too far in their use of the rational/discursive mode of preaching,[3] I am of the belief that contemporary black preachers do not go far enough in setting forth a rational claim based on a sound interpretive strategy that opens the way for in-depth scriptural exegesis with a clearly defined focus or controlling thought. These components of the sermon-creation process should be evident before they turn to the type of celebration defined by Mitchell as "emotional rejoicing."[4] In more recent years, all-too-many black sermons have become more shallow and shrill as preachers go for the quick and cheap celebrative thrill to the neglect of more creative and sound exposition in their preaching. Preaching must do more than engage one's emotions; it must also lay a claim on one's heart, mind, and soul. That claim motivates us to live out our faith in what Don Saliers has described as God's "beautiful, terrifying world."[5] As has so often been said, when we enter the sanctuary to worship, we need not surrender our minds at the front door of the church, for in believing we can think, and in thinking we can believe. The main thrust of the black sermon must not rely on emotion alone to get a hearing. This is not to suggest that emotion has no place in black preaching, but the emotion must not come at the expense or neglect of the intellect and the will.[6] Marvin McMickle has observed that the much-ballyhooed verbal response in the black pew is not always an accurate barometer of whether or not the congregation has received the message. A more accurate response to the sermon's effectiveness, according to McMickle, could be "silent but rapt attention" that comes when something has been said that captures and holds the attention of the congregation.[7] It is indeed possible to engage the minds of black listeners without all the emotional hype that we have come to expect from the traditional celebratory preaching style.

Second, celebration used as a rhetorical tool places an undue burden on the preacher to close out each Sunday's sermon on a highly emotional note, often filled with loud voice and animated histrionics. Many black preachers who feel compelled to strive each Sunday for this "joyful and ecstatic reinforcement of the truth"[8] often struggle under the weight of what I describe as the "celebratory burden" to the neglect of the rest of the sermon. Some preachers say that they prepare their celebratory close even before they write the body of their sermon, for they view the manner in which they close their sermons as the most crucial part of their preaching. Both Mitchell and Thomas argue that the celebratory sermonic close is indeed where the focus should be.[9] Mitchell goes so far as to say that the body of the sermon is often best written after it becomes clear how the celebration will relate to the text and purpose. "This," says Mitchell, "helps to insure that the main body will be written to flow into a celebration that focuses on the purpose."[10] Thomas, agreeing with Mitchell concerning the importance of the sermon's celebratory ending, observes that even Martin Luther King Jr., in a conversation about the first steps of his sermon preparation, said, "The first thing I think about is how I'm going to close."[11] What Thomas fails to mention about King's comment, published by Wyatt Tee Walker in *The Soul of Black Worship,* is that Walker, to whom King made the remark, listed this climactic close as one of the superficial characteristics of black preaching.[12]

Many black preachers feel that they have been a failure in the pulpit if their sermons don't end on this high celebratory note each and every Sunday. In my twenty-five years as a professor of preaching it has often pained me to see black novice preachers—young and old alike—struggling to master this misguided understanding of celebration as a useful, and in some cases even necessary, rhetorical tool. It is especially disheartening when this desire takes precedent over substantive content in the sermon. Though whites and others outside of the black preaching tradition could learn much from the multiple styles of black oratory, this celebratory burden is an expectation that most of their beginning preachers do not labor under when trying to master the basics of sermon preparation.[13] This overemphasis on celebrating—especially for young black preachers—could be a deterrent to their development as sound biblical exegetes, whose first concern should be to make sure they've made that vital connection between a fitting explication of

Scripture, paired with a keen insight into lived experience, and an ever-deepening understanding of the ways in which effective preaching, as a gift from God, nourishes the life of the church.[14]

Moreover, when the celebratory close involves "whooping"—the preacher's sing-song chanting of the sermon[15]—it places an additional burden on preachers who feel awkward engaging in such oratorical gymnastics or who feel they simply don't have the gifts to master such techniques in their preaching.[16] In the opening years of this twenty-first century some notable seminary-trained and untrained ministers alike have reenergized the whooping style and taken it to new heights, using its popular appeal to draw hundreds of black congregants to their worship services on Sunday morning.[17] The renewed popularity of the "neo-whooper" places an undue burden on preachers who long for that type of numerical success in their ministries and who erroneously believe that whooping is the only way to achieve it even when they know they don't have the oratorical gifts to scale such rhetorical heights.[18]

Many times this very pronounced style of celebration—defined in another instance as "climactic utterance"[19]—places an additional weight on African American women preachers, who must decide 1) whether or not to imitate the celebratory close of men, 2) develop some form of whooping more fitting for women, 3) totally ignore the celebrative impulse, or 4) simply close out their sermons feeling that they have not quite measured up to the expectations of the celebratory black preaching tradition.[20] Unrealistic celebratory expectations make it difficult for women to find their own voices in a male-dominated clerical order. Untold numbers of women still have to fight for their right to be heard as ministers of the gospel in many predominantly black congregations. The expectation that they will also celebrate in styles similar to men becomes another hurdle for them to overcome. Growing numbers of women are opting out of traditional black churches and heading to denominations that are more open to their pastoral gifts and callings. Among those gifts are their more nuanced preaching styles. Whether they recognize it or not, traditional black churches are suffering a leadership brain drain as black women exit the black church in ever-increasing numbers for denominations and congregations that are more receptive to their ways of preaching, which often do not include the celebratory whoop.

Third, using celebration as a rhetorical tool at times seems to encourage the listening congregation to exude a pasted, superficial joy, whether it is heartfelt or not. Some years ago I recall a vice president of the National Baptist Convention, USA leaving the auditorium one night where the national meeting was held, bitterly complaining about how tired he was after having goaded the congregation into "celebrating" the featured minister's less-than-stellar sermon. He confessed that he had exerted more energy than the guest preacher as he tried to force the people to engage in celebratory call-and-response. On other occasions when a congregation is not verbally supportive of the preacher when he or she moves to the celebration part of the sermon, some preachers have been known to ask, "Can I get a witness?" or to look up at the ceiling and say, "Amen lights," indicating that the response they are hearing from the congregation is not sufficient to the celebratory preaching that is being done. In such instances one is hard pressed not to conclude that what is being sought is not worshipful praise that rightly belongs to God but a "celebrative lift" for the preacher.

A celebrative lift happens when the congregation responds vocally to the urgings of the minister to join in the celebration he or she is trying to evoke through rhetoric. Many times members of the congregation respond with "Amen!" "Yes!" "Come on now," or "Stay up with her, church!" This lift is intended to help the preacher over his or her "homiletical hump" when the sermon lacks life and energy on its own. Though well-intentioned, celebrative lifts do not qualify as worshipful praise since they are directed toward humans and not toward God. This canned, manufactured joy can lead black worshipers to engage in what Annie Dillard calls our "surface meetings with God,"—where our worship becomes more anthropocentric (human) than theocentric (divine).[21] Whether heartfelt or not, many people in the congregation have come to believe that they are expected to act in a certain way near the close of the sermon based on the intonation, inflection, and rhythmic pace in the preacher's voice and pulpit manner. Such an expectation does not necessarily lead to authentic praise and adoration of God but at times can lead to empty ritual and contrived ceremony. This is especially true when the preacher has purposely sought to evoke this type of response in the congregation. Subjective feelings and on-demand antiphonal feedback are not the sole determinants of the efficacy of our joyous praise. Heartfelt praise glorifies God; pretentious praise does not.

Fourth, celebration as useful rhetoric focuses too much attention on the preacher and sets up what Charles Rice refers to as a tension between sacramental community and heroic individualism. In too many of our churches, according to Rice, people go to church to hear the Reverend So-and-So, and on infrequent Communion Sundays (when the Eucharist is celebrated) they stay away. These churches center, more or less, on a personality, and preaching is in many cases the means of perpetuating this situation. The results, says Rice, are idiosyncratic sermons, emphasis on issues and causes that may have only marginal connection with the gospel, undue promotionalism, a parochial moral and ethical perspective, and the self-serving, single-issue diatribe.[22] John Malcus Ellison, a former president of Virginia Union University, also argued for the centering of God and the decentering of the preacher in the preaching moment:

> The [preachers] who help people understand eternal verities and God's presence in human experience must do so soberly.... When the preacher is intellectually serious and evinces warmth of personality, a sense of the nearness and reality of God's presence seems to fill the atmosphere.... Worshipers then know that in religious services God is central. That is the end of all worship. That is the supreme purpose of all preaching and of all preparation for preaching. The sensational dramatist in the pulpit destroys the sense of worship because [he] makes himself central instead of God.[23]

An undue focus on the personality and emotive skills of the preacher can cause a congregation to lose sight of the object of worship—God!

Fifth, celebration as mere rhetorical device eventually affects the content of what is proclaimed in black preaching. Out of a desire to scale the celebratory heights Sunday in and Sunday out, preachers return again and again to what works in terms of getting the congregation emotionally excited. This is accomplished through oft-repeated anecdotes, illustrations totally detached from the main argument of the sermon, embellished tearjerkers devoid of truth, fanciful stories that tug at the emotions of congregants, or, when all else fails, a pyrotechnic pulpit display from a desperate preacher who has decided to mimic the celebration he or she has tried to evoke in the listeners. Sadly, in many congregations, what *works*, in terms of getting the people up on their feet, has often come to mean an empty, endless recitation of what Jesus accomplished on the cross of Calvary. Some ministers absolutely insist on preaching about the cross each Sunday as they prepare to close their sermon. The deeper theological depths of God's salvific work on the cross are seldom probed beyond the surface of that emotional, rhetorical flourish sought after at the close of the sermon. The preachers who feel compelled to close out their sermons in this way cheapen our understanding of the cross instead of leading us into a deeper knowledge of what God has done for us and for our salvation in Jesus Christ. The mere recitation of the crucifixion narrative every Sunday does not necessarily deepen our theological understanding of the cross.

Sixth, an unwarranted focus on a celebrative close can also lead to preaching devoid of any understanding of lament. In all too many of our churches there is a paucity of truthful reflection on the full range of our human existence. A word of hope for the suffering and sorrow that so many congregants face on a daily basis in a fallen world seems to elude any number of contemporary preachers who only want to preach "happy texts" or "gospel-lite" sermons that are more likely to elicit a shout of approval.[24] Otis Moss in *Blue Note Preaching* warns against this type of sermonizing when he calls on black preachers to recover the Blues sensibility in their preaching:

> America is living stormy Monday, but the pulpit is preaching happy Sunday. The world is experiencing the Blues, and pulpiteers are dispensing excessive doses of non-prescribed prosaic sermons with severe ecclesiastical and theological side effects. The Blues has faded from the Afro-Christian tradition, and the tradition is now lost in the clamor of material blessings, success without work, prayer without public concern, and preaching without burdens.[25]

Barbara A. Holmes in *Joy Unspeakable* notes the lack of lament in black churches even during Holy Week:

> On the day before Christ is betrayed, the contemplative dirge is de rigueur in many Eurocentric churches. But the atmosphere in most black churches remains inexorably joyful. Calls for solemnity rarely reign in the congregational need for catharsis. Perhaps we are still too historically close to actual lament to embrace its ritual counterpart.[26]

There can be no healing of the vagaries and vicissitudes of life that afflict so many people that does not begin with the sober recognition of our brokenness and our desperate desire to be healed.[27] When we look at the psalms of lamentation it becomes clear that true worship is not limited to celebration, nor is it spoiled by tears of lament.[28] Luke Powery states that while homiletics has recognized celebration as a work of the Spirit in preaching, the same has not been true for lament. He argues that we must see both as works of the Spirit.[29] Sally Brown, in an effort to reclaim *biblical* lament in preaching, notes that congregations unfamiliar with biblical lament will lack the rhetorical, psychological, or theological resources for honest engagement with God in the face of trouble:

> At the heart of gospel preaching stands the cross. Christian hope is anchored in a God who has entered utterly into suffering and grief. News of grace and resurrection rings hollow disconnected from daily realities of loss, dispossession, and yearning for justice. Testifying to the God of Easter requires the language of lament.[30]

An overemphasis on celebration could cause the black pulpit to shy away from articulating the language of lament, skimming over or outright denying the reality of suffering and brokenness in our communities. Jamie Grant observes in *Worshipping Trinity* that neither hope of Christ nor certainty of ultimate divine resolution to our problems in any way denies the need for human lament:

> Lament is not based on the psalmist's lack of future hope; lament is grounded in the psalmist's *present* experience of life with God in the world. Lament is intrinsic to humanity living in relationship with God in his good *but fallen* world. . . . The knowledge that everything will be alright does not change the fact that, in our humanity, we need to respond before God to those present realities that are not alright.[31]

While every sermon should carry good news, every sermon needs a Good Friday move where one takes seriously the ravages and perils of living in a fallen world groaning for redemption. A sermon that always ends in celebration (emotional rejoicing) can become a mere whistling past the graveyard or, even worse, the celebration of our captivity to a homiletic gone astray.

Moreover, Mitchell and Thomas are too inclined to equate noncelebratory preaching with hell-fire-and-brimstone condemnation as if to suggest that a sermon that does not end in celebration must of necessity end in hopelessness.[32] This does not necessarily have to be the case. Good news does not always sound good *to* us, but if it is indeed good news, it can be good *for* us. Sometimes preaching involves a word of correction, admonition, warning, exhortation, judgment, and so forth. There are any number of times when the sermon should leave us in a sober, reflective, thought-provoking mood as we ponder the exigencies and challenges of life in the full knowledge that God has promised never to leave us nor forsake us (e.g., the penitential psalms). Sometimes hope and promise are best heard when a congregation believes the preacher has taken the gravity of their plight seriously. Some sermons simply don't call for a demonstrative celebration at the end. Thinking that all sermons should end in emotional rejoicing could conceivably lead black preachers away from more content-filled, sober reflections on the Word of God. Insisting on a celebratory close could cause the preacher to become a one-note Johnny as every sermon *must* end in celebration with an often premature triumphalist claim to victory tacked on for good measure. Preachers need to be reminded that there is ambiguity, open-endedness, and paradox in the best of preaching if we take Paul's admonition seriously: "For now we see in a mirror, dimly, but then we will see face to face" (1 Cor. 13:12). No preacher can say or settle it all in one sermon. Preaching the whole counsel of God requires us to deal with a wide array of human situations and emotions, all of which can end on a hopeful note, though not necessarily a happy, effervescent, or bubbly one.

I am not suggesting that the problems created by our present-day misunderstandings of celebration as useful rhetoric as opposed to worshipful praise are the sole responsibility of Mitchell and Thomas. Transcribed black sermons from the eighteenth and nineteenth centuries, along with recorded black sermons from the twentieth century known as race records, will show the powerful role emotion has played in black preaching long before the publishing careers of either of these men.[33] What I am arguing is that celebration as a useful rhetorical tool, separate and apart from an understanding of its doxological and liturgical roots, must be critiqued lest the celebratory aspects of black worship and preaching degenerate into meaningless cultural rituals (festivity) that take away from rather than add to the depths and richness of our worshipful praise that comes from our longed-for encounter with transcendence.

Mitchell and Thomas, with their celebration homiletic that focuses too intently on the ending of the sermon, are in need of a more in-depth understanding of the place of doxology in preaching, out of which a right understanding of celebration as worshipful praise should come. In actuality, their homiletic is not primarily celebratory in a theological sense, but it is so in a cultural sense, which is to say, their definitions of *celebration* are primarily derived from socio-cultural understandings of festivity and not from theology. Their homiletic basically consists of two parts. In the first instance, they have constructed an affective homiletic that is intended to appeal to the emotions. By affective, I mean that they have built their homiletic around an experiential/intuitive construct in the belief that people remember and do what reaches them emotionally (affectively) in the collection of core belief. They define "core belief" as "broad principles for living shaped by cognitive, emotive, and intuitive evaluation of life and experience."[34]

A homiletic that moves beyond the cognitive to include the emotive and intuitive can indeed be a viable homiletic.[35] However, the problem arises when Mitchell and Thomas attempt to implement the second part of their homiletic—a celebratory close intended to provide ecstatic reinforcement to their affective (experiential) sermonic approach. They unsuccessfully attempt to tie a theologically deficient, cultural understanding of celebration to the emotion they have sought to engender through their affective homiletic. Their efforts to attach celebration to their affective homiletic causes their homiletic to go astray because the definitions they use to describe *celebration* have been detached from or are lacking in traditional theological and doxological understandings of the term—praise given in ritual worship that has God as its aim and end.[36] Their lack of a solid theological definition begs the question: If the celebration they espouse in worship and preaching is not praise offered to God in its most fundamental sense, then who and what are they celebrating?

Not only do Mitchell and Thomas detach celebration from its theological roots; they then assign to it a preeminent pedagogical function to the neglect of its long-standing doxological importance. Even though both scholars have sections in their books on a "theology of celebration," their definitions don't define celebration per se but merely describe how celebration functions in their homiletic while a more in-depth discussion of a theology of praise and the various ways in which ritual praise finds expression in preaching is minimized or nonexistent. A right understanding of praise would anchor their celebration in a fitting theological construction that would not be overly dependent on rhetoric to carry the day. Their detachment of celebration from theology and their prioritizing of these ritual acts as a pedagogical function skew the celebration called forth in their homiletic toward an embellished rhetorical act with minimal doxological (praise) significance. Thus, the celebratory portion of their two-pronged homiletic ends up having the same effect on black preaching that the wrestling angel had on Jacob at the River Jabbok—it blesses and cripples at the same time (Gen. 32:22–32). It blesses because blacks have historically understood that when the word of God is proclaimed, heard, and received, it is right to give God our thanks and praise. But it also cripples because it is the functional import of celebration—how it helps us to remember and to do—that is really at the heart of the celebratory portion of their homiletic, not the worshipful praise of God that attends our preaching when we have understood the manner in which this God who is present in the preaching moment has accommodated Godself through God's mighty acts, the nourishment of the church, and the building up of the church's wider witness to the world. It is the latter understanding of celebration that should be the aim and end of our preaching, and there should be a fitting theological understanding there to guide it.

When this ritual act of celebration no longer has the praise of God at its center, it defaults often to a rhetorical function in which the structuring of words and the heat of emotion try to guarantee the presence of effectual praise when in actuality it is the gift of the Spirit that enables humans truly to worship God.[37] When functional rhetoric replaces praise, our words are inclined to be, in the words of Shakespeare, "full of sound and fury signifying nothing."[38] Also, when one attempts to preach a sermon where the praise of God is dethroned and rhetoric is enthroned, this loss of a theological understanding of celebration often turns the most well-intentioned celebratory rhetoric to anthropocentric whims and desires that focus on the needs and wants of individuals and not on the praise of the God who is for us! Mitchell's and Thomas's understanding of celebration as emotional rejoicing or ecstatic reinforcement takes the eyes of both preachers and congregants off the right praise of God, off the bivalent nature of adoration and action, and also off the manner in which the church is built up through preaching as gift of the Spirit. "Preaching," according to John Calvin, "is essential since its offer of Christ via the collaboration of the Spirit is the means by which the church is built up."[39] A functional celebration, erroneously claiming to build up the church—that is, people remember and do what they celebrate—causes us to end up with a feel-good religion but not a very deep faith. What we desperately need is a clear understanding of celebration, first and foremost, as worshipful praise. For that we must turn to the theory out of which present-day understandings of celebration originated.

4
Festivity Theory and the Origins of Celebration

Celebration is at the heart of Mitchell's and Thomas's affective homiletic, so it is important to understand how they define and use the word *celebration*. Mitchell provides several definitions: "emotional rejoicing," "getting emotional about something," "ecstatic reinforcement," "joyous praise," or "purposefully focused emotional expression."[1] Thomas defines *celebration* as "The culmination of the sermonic design, where a moment is created in which the remembrance of a redemptive past and/or the conviction of a liberated future transforms the events immediately experienced."[2] In another instance, quoting from Mitchell, Thomas defines *celebration* as "climactic utterance."[3] These definitions, for the most part, detach the word *celebration* from its historical and theological antecedents.[4] Though they may qualify as general definitions, with respect to the worship of God, they lack a firm grounding in theology.[5]

Historically and in contemporary times, the mere act of celebrating can be but is not necessarily religious in its orientation.[6] Victor Turner observes that to celebrate is essentially to perform public and formal rituals.[7] Understood as such, *celebration* can be defined in any number of ways:

1. To observe (a day or event) with ceremonies of respect, festivity, or rejoicing
2. To perform publicly and duly (e.g., a religious ceremony or a distinguished career)

3. To honor or praise publicly (e.g., a person of achievement or a sonnet that celebrates love)
4. To engage in festivities (secular and/or religious)[8]

Though the word *celebration* can carry a wide range of meanings, when it is used to refer to Christian worship, it needs a theological foundation.[9] Festivity theorists on the order of Josef Pieper claim that the celebratory rituals performed by Christians in their worship settings have contained some understanding of celebration as the worshipful praise of God.[10] One must thus make a distinction between *festivity* as referring to cultural phenomena and *celebration* as a label for religious ritual even though the words are closely related to one another. *Festivity* is often defined as mere joy and revelry (cultural) while *celebration*, in the religious realm, may be defined as acts of worshipful praise (sacred) that often include joy and revelry, especially in many African American churches.

FESTIVITY

Festivity in its various forms and expressions has been a long-standing feature of the African American sociocultural experience. In fact, Harvey Cox rightly notes in *Feast of Fools* that all humans are essentially festive and ritual creatures. But Cox further notes that African Americans possess a more festive and feeling-oriented approach to life often referred to as *soul*.[11] *Celebration*, the catch-all word we often use to describe this soulful festivity in its various expressions, had its origins in the observance of ancient festivals. Cox defines *festivity* as a socially approved occasion for the expression of feelings that are normally repressed or neglected.[12] Humans are by nature creatures who not only work and think but who sing, dance, pray, tell stories, and celebrate. Festivity is a common ingredient in the human condition, and no culture is without it. According to Cox, when festivity disappears from a culture, something universally human is lost.[13] Festivity is literally a time to let it all hang out! Cox adds that anyone who possesses the capacity for genuine revelry and joyous celebration can be said to be participating in some form of festivity. Among African Americans, history shows that even during the dark days of slavery, and often to the amazement of the dominant culture, slaves engaged in extended periods of festivity. Historian Leon Litwack in *Been in the Storm So Long* notes that near the end of the Civil War, on hearing the news that Union General W.

T. Sherman's troops had moved into South Carolina, a white family witnessed their slaves' festivities with mixed feelings:

> We have been watching the Negroes dancing for the last two hours. Mother had the partition taken down in our old house so that they have quite a long ball room. We can sit on the piazza and look into it. I hear now the sounds of fiddle, tambourine, and "bones" mingled with the shuffling and pounding of feet. Mr. Axley is fiddling for them. They are having a merry time, thoughtless creatures, they think not of the morrow.[14]

Those slaves were hardly thoughtless creatures unconcerned with tomorrow. The news that Union troops were near and the hope that their freedom would soon follow caused them to disavow their normally repressed feelings and to engage freely in a festive moment with their singing, dancing, and revelry. They were engaged in the type of festivity that Cox describes as the full recognition that tragedy, brutality, chaos, failure, and death are essential parts of the glory of humankind. They knew that their festive celebrations, rather than a retreat from the reality of injustice and evil, occurred most authentically where these negative realities were recognized and tackled. Their festivity stemmed not from ignorance, thoughtlessness, or a lack of concern about their plight but rather from a joyous confidence in the ultimate goodness of life and in their ability to survive the evils of slavery.[15] It was their time to engage in excess and chaos and to say yes to life even in the face of the harsh realities of slavery.

Philosopher Josef Pieper, in his work *In Tune with the World*, identifies five traits that are essential to festivity: exceptionality, free activity, contemplation, celebratory joy, and excess. Cox, who draws heavily on Pieper's work, conflates and narrows these essential ingredients of festivity to three:[16] (1) conscious excess, (2) celebratory affirmation, and (3) juxtaposition.

Conscious Excess

By conscious excess, Cox understands festive activity as revelry. "We always 'overdo it,' and we do so on purpose. We 'live it up.' We stay up later, eat and drink more, and spend more money than we ordinarily would. Perhaps we laugh or cry or both."[17] For a festive occasion, says Cox, we also dress up:

Sometimes we wear things that would be stared at curiously or disapprovingly on most occasions: funny hats, tuxedos, daring dresses, exotic shirts; in some circles, even rows of medals and crimson sashes. We clothe ourselves, that is, with calculated excess.[18]

Many African Americans, religious and nonreligious alike, will be able to identify with Cox's example of excessive dress for festive occasions. One need only call to mind some of the regalia worn by both male and female African American congregants on Sunday mornings to know that this aspect of festivity—calculated excess—is still in vogue in black culture and black religion.[19] Traditionally blacks worshiped God in the beauty of their best apparel, for they wanted their clothes to reflect God's own glory.[20] Though dress-down days are becoming more common in black churches, many blacks continue to approach God in the splendor of their dress, outwardly embodying the claim that they are meant to be God's own well-clothed royalty, enjoying the marriage feast of the lamb in style.[21] Thus Sunday is still regarded in many circles as the day for blacks to dress up.[22] This festive component of chaos and excess is not only seen at religious observances like the Sunday morning worship hour but also at funerals, banquets, conferences, parties, family reunions, or any other time when festivity is in order. Festivity provides a short vacation from convention, and without elements of socially approved infraction of the norms of ordinary behavior, festivity would not be festivity.[23] Cox, quoting from Pieper's *In Tune with the World*, notes that a festival embraces the moment: "It is in no way tied to other goals; it has been removed from all 'so that' and 'in order to.'" In festive *excess*, says Pieper, we delight in the here and now, putting out of our minds for the moment the fact that we have to get up for work tomorrow or that we may be overtaxing our legs or our digestive tracts.[24]

A festival is essentially a phenomenon of existential richness, adds Pieper. Lavishness is one of its elements. Thus, every festival conceals within itself at least a germ of excess; it contains what appears to some as a senseless and excessive waste of the yield of work, an extravagance that violates all rationality.[25] The festival is a way to say no to those who try to inflict their worship of work on the rest of the world.[26] In a world governed by work, the person who is limited to utilitarian activity or unable to engage in excess has rightly been called unfestive. On the other hand, voluntary renunciation of the yield of a working day cuts through the principle of calculating utility. Even in conditions of extreme material scarcity, the withholding from work, in the midst of a life normally governed by work, creates an area of free surplus—excess![27] Excess is a trait of festivity blacks along with others have long enjoyed.

Celebrative Affirmation

Festivity, according to Cox, also involves celebrative affirmation—"saying yes to life." It is a broad, vibrant, robust yes that includes joy in the deepest sense. It may be affirmation because of something that has happened, like a new job or a diploma, or it may celebrate something that is still only hoped for. It may even be the celebration that occurs partly in spite of something that has happened. At such times we affirm life and gaiety despite the facts of failure and death.[28] In a religious context celebration that says yes to life even in the face of failure and bitter disappointments calls to mind the biblical passage in Hab. 3:17–19:

> Though the fig tree does not blossom,
>   and no fruit is on the vines;
> though the produce of the olive fails,
>   and the fields yield no food;
> though the flock is cut off from the fold,
>   and there is no herd in the stalls,
> yet I will rejoice in the LORD;
>   I will exult in the God of my salvation.
> God, the Lord, is my strength;
>   he makes my feet like the feet of a deer,
> and makes me tread upon the heights.

In a secular context, the extravagant New Orleans funerals modeled after the West African custom of enlisting musicians to accompany the deceased to his or her final resting place is a prime example of celebrative affirmation in the face of and in spite of death.[29] Beginning in the eighteenth century, black funeral musicians adopted American military band instruments—drums, tubas, and trumpets—to serenade the spirit of the deceased. They dressed in quasi-military apparel with smart-looking caps, white shirts, and dark pants:

> A traditional [New Orleans] funeral always began the same way, with the band assembling in the morning, then beginning with stately slow numbers, a few hymns, and the inevitable "Flee as a Bird" to accompany the deceased to his grave; this was a soft, lilting

lament mingling sadness and the release from mortal cares. These brass bands resembled the Salvation Army marching for the glory of Temperance, but the resemblance ended there. Although the New Orleans brass bands played their music soberly and respectfully at the start of a funeral, they soon allowed the rites to take wing and to become a dancing, singing celebration.[30]

The singing and carousing that accompanied the New Orleans funeral was their secular expression of celebrative affirmation. Even in the face of death they were able to express their deep joy over the life that had been so recently among them. They said yes to life and death not just through the somber music of a typical funeral rite but also through the upbeat notes of the funeral parade. Though the musicians who accompanied the deceased to their graves in the New Orleans funerals often performed their services in a sacred context, those who participated were not necessarily religious themselves. Nor did they attach any religious significance to their participation in the band. Harvey Cox notes that jazz, that most secular form of music made famous by black musicians, in one form at least, was born in the black church and was first played in connection with black funeral services.[31] Those who played in the band as well as those who enjoyed the music of the band were not always associated with religion, but they had a deep feel for the inherent qualities of the festive. Thus they affirmed life and death through their celebratory music. They had no trouble moving from dirge to dance; from life to death.

Juxtaposition

Juxtaposition, Cox's third characteristic of the festive, is related to festivity in the sense that festivity must display contrast, which is to say, it must be noticeably different from "everyday life." Even though many children wish Christmas could come every day, part of the appeal of Christmas comes because it occurs only once a year. Thus it is appropriate, says Cox, that holidays are printed in red on the calendar since the festive quality of a holiday depends on its being exceptional. It is not the norm; it exists in juxtaposition to the norm, thus heightening its unusual festive quality. Festivity, however, cannot be reduced merely to the unusual. It is not *just* not working; it also includes celebrative affirmation and excess, as previously mentioned.[32] The reality of festivity depends on an alternation with the everyday schedule of work, convention, and moderation. The festive quality of any event depends on its exceptional nature.[33] It works its wonder both in religion and culture; in the sacred and the secular. Wyatt Tee Walker draws a distinction between the sacred and the secular in the celebratory dance moment by saying that when one moves from side to side, it is secular, but when one jumps up and down, it is sacred![34]

In summary, festivity is a time set aside for the full expression of feelings. It consists of an irreducible element of prodigality, of "living it up." Moreover, it says yes to lived experience and embraces joy, which explains why we wish people happiness on holidays and consider a party successful when "a good time was had by all." Festivity, as something we do for its own sake, provides us with a short vacation from the daily round, an alternation without which life would be unbearable.[35]

Historically, the festival has been that special time when ordinary chores were set aside while humans celebrated some event, affirmed the sheer goodness of what is, or observed the memory of a god or hero. The festive spirit arises from humankind's peculiar power to incorporate into their lives the joys of other people and the experiences of previous generations. Festivity has also been understood as a human form of play, through which humans appropriated an extended area of life, including the past, into their own experience.[36] Humans are by their very nature a festive people because the festive draws a much-needed distinction between the routine of our workday world and free activity.[37] While work is an everyday occurrence, festive activity is something special, unusual, an interruption in the ordinary passage of time. Josef Pieper argues that "the idle rich" (*dolce vita*) are hard put to engage in festivity since only meaningful work can provide the soil in which festivity flourishes.[38] Festivity, with its essential ingredients—excess, celebration, and juxtaposition—is itself an essential ingredient in human life.[39]

CELEBRATION AS WORSHIPFUL PRAISE

Our understanding of festivity must be nuanced, however, when we move into the realm of the sacred, for then it becomes more than mere excess, affirmation, and contrast. Probing into the depths of festivity theory allows us to distinguish festivity as mere joy and revelry from festivity that embraces the sacred. While the festive shows up repeatedly in black culture as well as in other cultures, the sacred dimension is not always readily apparent. Pieper and other festivity theorists argue that the sacred festival always involves more than merely having a good time. Take, for example, the funeral parades in New Orleans. Although they became an established part of the religious rites of passage from life to death, the parade itself and the preparations leading up to it—during which participants had a good time eating, drinking, shouting, and "rocking the coffin" the night before—was not necessarily a worshipful act. Instead, it accompanied and/or stood in juxtaposition to a religious ritual. The funeral parade was filled with revelry but not necessarily worshipful praise.[40] Festivity alone is not sufficient to usher us into the worshipful presence of God.

A distinction has to be made between celebration as mere revelry and celebration as worshipful praise. Although Cox draws heavily on Pieper's understanding of festivity, he leaves out two of Pieper's festivity traits that point specifically to the sacred—contemplation and celebratory joy. Pieper argues that the concept of festivity is inconceivable without an element of contemplation.[41] Historically, contemplation of the unchangeable order of things and of its divine origin has been the highest possible human activity—it was considered the activity of the divine in human beings.[42] The festival in its deeper understanding is an event set aside for the contemplation of divine things. Festivals are more than mere joy and revelry; they help us to see God and the ways of God more intimately and insightfully. According to Pieper, the traditional name for the utmost perfection to which humans attain the fulfillment of their being is *visio beatifica*—the "seeing that confers bliss." This highest intensification of life, which true festivity helps us to enter into, takes place as a kind of spiritual seeing that has value and worth beyond empirical knowledge. It is an awareness of the divine ground of the universe.[43] This kind of happiness takes place in contemplation, when one reflects on the goodness of God and God's creation. According to Pieper, "Whenever anyone succeeds in bringing before the mind's eye the hidden ground of everything that is, they succeed to the same degree in performing an act that is meaningful in itself. The result is that they have a good time."[44] A union of peace, intensity of life, and contemplation are essential for festivity, so that to celebrate a festival is equivalent to "becoming contemplative, and in this state, directly confronting the higher realities (divine things) on which the whole of existence rests."[45] The challenge for people of faith is to move celebration from mere festivity to the deeper understanding of worshipful praise.

The second trait that moves festivity closer to the sacred is celebratory joy. Of this trait Pieper said, "On a festival day people enjoy themselves. An early Christian Greek went so far as to say, 'Festivity is joy and nothing else.'"[46] However, Pieper argues that joy is a secondary phenomenon:

> No one can rejoice absolutely for joy's sake alone.... Nevertheless, the longing for joy is nothing but the desire to have a reason and pretext for joy. This reason, to the extent that it actually exists, precedes joy and is different from it. The reason comes first and the joy comes second.[47]

Pieper maintains that the reason for joy, although it may be encountered in a thousand concrete forms, is always the same: possessing or receiving what one loves, whether actually in the present, hoped for in the future, or remembered in the past. Joy, according to Pieper, is an expression of love and is most deeply felt when one is in tune and in touch with the divine. One who loves nothing and nobody cannot possibly rejoice, no matter how desperately he or she craves joy. Joy is the response of a lover receiving what he or she loves.[48] It was Chrysostom who stated this characteristic of festivity most clearly: *Ubi caritas gaudet, ibi est festivitas*—"Where love rejoices, there is festivity."[49] This deepest expression of joy comes to us as a gift from the creator God.

Our love of celebration and the joy that emanates from it come to us out of historical understandings of festivity. The five festive traits listed by Pieper: exceptionality, free activity, contemplation, excess, and celebratory joy constitute the framework for our present-day understandings of celebration, but they also point us to the deeper sacred meanings of celebration. From antiquity forward, the act of celebrating grows out of and is linked to aspects of festivity, and festivity has in turn been linked to the sacred. Sociologists and anthropologists have long understood each of these two terms—*celebration* and *festivity*—as being essential to each other.[50] In fact, according to Allesandro Falassi, a *festival* may be defined as a sacred or profane time of celebration, marked by special observances.[51] Roger Caillois moves the festival closer to a religious orientation by arguing that in reality the festival was often regarded as the dominion of the sacred: "The day of the festival, the Sabbath, is first of all a day consecrated to the divine, on which work is forbidden, on which one must rest, rejoice, and praise God."[52]

Not only has the sacred been historically linked to festivals, but Pieper argues emphatically that secular as well as religious festivals have their roots in the rituals of worship.[53] According to Pieper, a definition for *festival* included in the collected works of Plato and fully accepted by Cicero and the people of ancient Rome contained a simple but terse phrase: *heiros chronos*—"holy time." The people of antiquity regarded the festival as a holy day.[54] Linked to this holy time has been this deeper understanding of celebration as the worshipful praise of God. Pieper argues that one could not conceive a more intense, more unconditional affirmation of being and lauding of the Creator than worshipful praise.[55] He believes that it was this desire to affirm God and the world—expressing itself in praise, glorification, and thanksgiving for the whole of reality and existence—that has prompted acts of celebration in festivity and in Christian worship.[56] Richard Lischer points out that the word *praedicare*, which we now associate with preaching, at one time meant "to praise," or "to celebrate."[57] Even the act of preaching has its roots in worshipful praise.

On the basis of the above-mentioned beliefs concerning festivity and the sacred, we may logically conclude that religious observances involving celebration have historically included a theological understanding of the word. Our celebratory acts must be lodged within a genuine theology of praise where our thoughts and actions are offered to God in worshipful praise and not merely in revelry.[58] When celebration is understood in this light, our ritual acts have a deeper meaning than mere emotion, emotional rejoicing, or ecstatic reinforcement.[59] If the celebration that is often identified with black preaching is merely festive, then the highly anticipated climactic closing of the black sermon could simply be joy and revelry, but if it carries the deeper understanding of festivity espoused by Caillois and Pieper, then it moves into the realm of the sacred as worshipful praise and must be defined more broadly than mere emotional rejoicing. The display of emotion and animated histrionics often seen in the black pulpit and pew may not be a sign of worshipful praise but could simply be an expression of the long-standing traits of festivity. Without a doubt blacks generally have a joyful time in worship, but joyful times don't necessarily translate into praise. Festivity that does not embrace the sacred, even when it happens within the context of worship, may well involve revelry and rejoicing characterized by excess and contrast, but that rejoicing does not necessarily translate into worshipful praise that rightly belongs to God.

THE FUNCTION OF CELEBRATION

Having argued for a nuanced theological understanding of celebration as worshipful praise and not mere festivity involving joy and revelry, we must now address Mitchell's and Thomas's claims about the functional purposes of celebration. It is Thomas who most clearly ties the ending of the sermon to a functional purpose: "Celebration in the final stage of the sermon functions as the joyful and ecstatic reinforcement of the truth already taught and delivered in the main body of the sermon."[60] Intentionally or not, Mitchell and Thomas take a less-than-theological understanding of celebration (revelry and emotional rejoicing) and put it to use in service to the sermon. In so doing they turn what should be a preeminent act of praise into a mostly pedagogical function.

Mitchell and Thomas use their quasi-theological understanding of celebration to bring functional, emotional fire power to the sermon. This focus on function tends to suggest that the only time praise takes place in worship is at an emotionally charged rhetorical level near the end of the sermon. It also suggests that people who don't engage in this type of celebration may in some way be missing the mark of effectual praise in the preaching and hearing of the word of God.

In a manner of speaking, Mitchell and Thomas give their celebratory praise a job to do and justify it by claiming that people will only remember and do from the sermon what they celebrate and get emotional about.[61] They use evocative rhetoric at the climactic close of their sermons primarily to influence the behavior of people and to serve as a positive reinforcement of the gospel.[62] Mitchell argues forcefully that what we get emotional about we retain far longer; thus celebration is the best way to motivate people to *do* the will of God.[63] But the primary task of true praise is the glorification of God. The Westminster Catechism teaches that [humankind's] chief end is to glorify God and to enjoy him forever,[64] but for Mitchell and Thomas the most important aspect of celebration is not necessarily its praiseworthiness but rather its functional use—it helps us to remember and to do what we hear in the sermon.[65] Mitchell and Thomas are right to suggest that praise should act in tandem with action, but the rhythm between the two is neither triggered nor provoked simply by way of embellished rhetoric purposely structured to evoke an emotional response in the listeners. There is no guarantee that emotionally laden speech that leads to celebration and emotional rejoicing is a necessary kick-start to action. Adoration and action are binary in nature and interact with each other on the basis of a right understanding of the work of the Spirit as it relates to service and praise.[66]

Miroslav Volf argues that Christian worship consists in both obedient service to God and in the joyful praise of God. Both of these elements are brought together in Heb. 13:15–16:

> Through him, then, let us continually offer a sacrifice of praise to God, that is, the fruit of lips that confess his name. Do not neglect to do good and to share what you have, for such sacrifices are pleasing to God.

Volf maintains that the sacrifice of praise and the sacrifice of good works are two fundamental aspects of the Christian way of "being-in-the-world."[67] They are at the same time the two constitutive elements of Christian worship: authentic Christian worship takes place in a rhythm of adoration and action. Adoration needs to take place as a distinct activity beside action because God did not create human beings to be merely God's servants but above all to be God's children and friends. As much as they need to do God's will in the world, says Volf, they need to enjoy God's presence also. The center of the Christian life consists in personal fellowship of human beings with the son of God through faith. Volf maintains that adoration is a time when this personal fellowship, which determines the whole life of Christians—their relation to themselves, to their neighbors, and to nature—is nurtured, either privately or corporately. This is the reason human beings need periodic moments of time in which God's commands concerning their work will disappear from the forefront of their consciousness as they adore the God of loving holiness and thank and pray to the God of holy love.

But, says Volf, because the world is God's creation and the object of God's redemptive purposes, we cannot make adoration our supreme goal, with action being a mere necessary consequence of adoration. Christian hope is not merely for the liberation of souls from the evil world. Hope redeems human beings and the world with which they comprise the good creation of God:

> The material creation is not a scaffolding that will be discarded once it has helped in the construction of the pure spiritual community of souls with one another and with God; material creation represents the building materials from which, after they are transfigured, the glorified world will be made. That is why worship can never be an

event taking place simply between the naked soul and its God. It must always include active striving to bring the eschatological new creation to bear on this world through the proclamation of the good news, nurture of the community of faith and socio-economic action. Fellowship with God is not possible without cooperation with God in the world; indeed cooperation with God is a dimension of fellowship with God.[68]

It is this two-dimensional hope that makes Christian worship a two-dimensional reality. Adoration and action are two distinct aspects of Christian worship, and each is valuable in its own right. The purpose of action is not merely to provide material support for the life of adoration, nor is the purpose of adoration simply to provide spiritual strength for the life of action. According to Volf, when we adore God, we worship God by enjoying God's presence and by celebrating God's mighty deeds of liberation. When we are involved in the world, we worship God by announcing God's liberation, and we cooperate with God by the power of the Spirit through loving action.

THE GIFT OF THE SPIRIT

Mitchell and Thomas are right to insist that adoration and action go hand in hand; however, they are in error when they maintain that highly emotional rhetoric is necessary to close the sermon because people will only remember and do what they celebrate (get emotional about). Celebratory rhetoric must not be viewed as the source or the required trigger for our action. We are not empowered to act by celebratory rhetoric or celebratory responses on the part of the people to the preacher's rhetoric. Rather, we are empowered by the Spirit—an empowerment that comes to us as gift. It is not something that we can earn, guarantee, or make happen on our own and most certainly not through an ostentatious display of our rhetorical skills. We engage in adoration and action only after we have received the gift of the Spirit.

According to Volf, action designates deeds that are directed toward the world while adoration designates words and symbolic actions that are directed toward God.

> This is why the writer of Hebrews can describe both the action and the adoration as "sacrifices": the one is a sacrifice of good works, the other a sacrifice of praise (see Heb. 13:15–16). As sacrifices, action

and adoration are something human beings give God. This is why both can properly be called "worship." For worship is something human beings owe God: in worship they are the givers, and God is the receiver.[69]

But as Volf rightly notes, our arms are lifeless and our mouths dumb if God does not give them the strength and facility of speech. We can give God only what we have first received from God. Thus, according to Volf, reception is a third dimension of Christian life that is even more fundamental than action or adoration. Christians are receivers in their new birth by the Holy Spirit, and that new life is sustained and flourishes only if they continue to be receivers throughout their Christian lives. The rhythm of adoration and action must be embedded in this larger rhythm consisting of passivity and activity.

The passivity of Christian existence can be described as receiving the Spirit by faith (which marks the beginning of Christian life; see Gal. 3:2) and being continually filled by the Spirit (which marks its continuation; see Eph. 5:18ff). The secret of the whole Christian life is passivity (receiving) in relation to the Spirit of God, for the Spirit, says Volf, is the source of both adoration and action. We rightly engage in both adoration and action when we receive the Spirit and are continually filled by the Spirit, not when we hear emotional rhetoric or ecstatic utterances. Our effectual praise should not be determined by our emotions or the pitch of our crafted speech but rather by our willingness to receive the Spirit, for we can only give to God and do in partnership with God what we have first received from God. It is our openness and receptivity to the Spirit that enables us to engage in adoration and action. People will remember and do what they have received from the Spirit, not simply what they have heard in celebratory rhetoric.

Luke Powery's *Spirit Speech* is helpful here, for Powery moves away from an overreliance on rhetoric to a fitting reliance on the Spirit in our acts of celebration and lament. Powery maintains that the presence of the Spirit can be discerned in sermon language, content, and structure. He further argues for five manifestations of the Spirit—lament, celebration, grace, unity, and fellowship. These five manifestations form Powery's theological-hermeneutical lens for discerning the presence of the Spirit in preaching while providing a theological language for speaking about the Spirit in relation to sermons.[70] In Powery's homiletic, adoration and action are the works of the Spirit and not merely of rhetoric and emotion.

In summary, celebratory praise is directed toward God in aim and intent and is much more than merely having a good time. Though such praise is closely related to revelry in the festive sense, it distinguishes itself through dependence on empowerment by the Spirit. While Mitchell and Thomas are right to insist that celebratory praise (adoration) and action are binary and go hand in hand, their overreliance on embellished rhetoric is much too dismissive of the work of the Spirit and the ways in which the Spirit initiates and empowers our adoration and action. Also, their claim that people will neither remember nor do what they do not celebrate is refuted in literally thousands of congregations across the United States and the world where demonstrative rhetoric is minimal or nonexistent but the work of God goes on in marvelous and mighty ways. There is a joyful ring to the word of God that does not need human embellishment in order to pierce the receptive hearts of the people of faith. It is the Spirit that empowers us to remember and to act, not ecstatic utterance or emotionally laden rhetoric at the climactic close of the sermon.

5
A Theology of Praise in Its Multiple Expressions

If celebration is not just revelry but praise, and if adoration and action come to us through the gift of the Spirit, then a theology of praise is crucial to a right understanding of one of the most creative moves in black preaching—the celebratory denouement. Praise can be defined as the human response to God's glory, power, mercy, and love. It consists largely of an acknowledgment or confession of God's existence and grandeur and the rendering of honor and glory to God:

> Praise is thus a response to the experience of God's grace and power and a proclamation that bears witness to that experience. It is also a primary human activity that occurs spontaneously and naturally. Praise is especially associated with joy, delight, jubilation, and a sense of wonder. Encountering the divine automatically gives rise to emotions such as awe, fear, desire, and exaltation. Praise attempts to articulate the feelings stirred by God's presence and power.[1]

Effectual praise in both the Old and New Testaments is neither coerced nor contrived but comes forth as a response to the experience of God's grace and power. It is often difficult to distinguish between praise, blessing, and thanksgiving in the Old Testament. The Hebrew verb used most often to mean "praise" is *hillel*. From this word is derived the English term *Alleluia* (from *Hallelu-yah*, "Praise Yahweh").[2] Hymns of praise were found throughout the ancient Near East, yet Israel's hymns were distinctive in that they were not manipulative.

They acknowledged the power and greatness of God, who had already accomplished wonderful things for the chosen people, but they did not attempt to flatter Yahweh in order to get something. Hymns of praise focus on God, not on humans. This understanding of praise debunks the oft-repeated mantra in black worship services: "When the praises go up, the blessings come down!" Our praise should acknowledge the power and greatness of God with no quid pro quo in mind. Thus that much beloved mantra should be dismissed for what it is: bad theology![3]

In the Old Testament the people of God were summoned into existence to be a people of God's own possession to make his praise "glorious" (Ps. 66:2). Verbs most often used of the worshiping people's approach to God—"to bow down" and "to serve"—are matched by other action words that tell us how pious Israelites thought of their offering of praise to the covenant God. Three verbs are expressive:

1. "To make noise" (Hebrew root, *halal*) underscores the obvious point that praise involves the use of words audibly expressed. Silent prayer is not a Hebrew practice; the reading of Scripture, on the other hand, is an exercise that involves the vocal chords (see Acts 8:30; Philip can hear the Ethiopian as he reads the prophetic writing).[4]
2. In a number of cases Yahweh's praise is celebrated by bodily movement and gesture. Singing and dancing (see Exod. 15:20–21; 1 Sam. 18:6; 2 Sam. 6:14) are part and parcel of this exuberant expression of praise (the verb "to praise" is taken from the Hebrew *yadah*, connected possibly with the hand [Heb. *yad*]; it means "to give thanks"). Thus for the psalmist one way in which God is exalted is with hands as well as voices upraised as a tribute of "thanksgiving."[5]
3. The verb *zamar* (in the form of *zimmer*, which the Greek Bible translates as *psallo*: "to sing hymns") covers musical activity, including the playing of instruments and singing in honor of Yahweh. The best translation is "to make melody." Individuals offer this type of praise, but choirs too may join their voices, as in the antiphonal responses of Psalm 136 and even more dramatically in Psalm 24. A variety of musical instruments is mentioned in Psalm 150:3–5, ranging from the trumpet blast and clashing cymbal to the sweet melody of flute and harp. All unite to "praise the LORD" (v.6).[6]

Praise is essentially the same in both the Old and New Testaments. In the New Testament, however, it is both confession and the rendering of honor and glory to God, but these now include the special role of Christ. The coming of the Messiah is an event for which both angels and human beings praise God (Luke 2:13–14, 20). In the New Testament the concepts of blessing, confession, honor, and glory are all closely related to praise and sometimes indistinguishable from it.

Praise can also be defined as an act of worship or acknowledgment by which the virtues or deeds of another are recognized and extolled. We praise God to express our joy to the Lord, both for who God is and for what God does (Ps. 150:2). Praising God for who God is, is called adoration; praising God for what God does is known as thanksgiving. Praise of God may be in song or prayer, individually or collectively, spontaneous or prearranged, originating from the emotions or from the will.[7] Frank Senn chooses to define praise in even more minute detail, drawing a distinction between praise as proclamation, thanksgiving, and adoration.[8] In defining praise as proclamation, Senn argues that we do not give praise to God only because God wants to be constantly affirmed but also to invite others to consider the wonders God has done and to respond appropriately. Thus, many of the classical hymns of the church are words of praise about God that we address to one another: for example, "Praise to the Lord, the Almighty," or "Now thank we all our God." With respect to praise as thanksgiving, Senn says that we give thanks not just to be polite but also because thanksgiving reinforces in us an awareness of the gifts of grace we receive from God. Indeed, in the act of thanksgiving we become aware that everything we receive from God in our created life, in our redemption through Christ, and in our sanctification by the Holy Spirit is a gift of grace. The highest moment of praise and thanksgiving in the church is the Great Thanksgiving or the Lord's Supper, which we sometimes call the Eucharist, from the Greek term for "thanksgiving." Finally, according to Senn, the act of the Eucharist leads to the third kind of praise—adoration—because Christ himself is present in, with, and through the bread and wine over which we give thanks. The act of Communion is surrounded by songs of adoration addressed to Christ.[9]

In the New Testament the chief emphasis falls on the praise Christian believers offer to God. *Aineo*—the word translated as "praise"—occurs eight times in the New Testament. It denotes the joyful praise of God expressed in doxology, hymn, or prayer, whether by individuals, the group of disciples, the community, or the angels.[10] Indeed, the raison d'etre of the church's life is to show forth the praises of God who has called the redeemed to himself. The life of praise is the hallmark of Christian existence because it demonstrates that the believing community has already anticipated the last day of God's final victory and is stretching out to share in its glories, even if the end is not yet attained.[11] Praise, therefore, according to Ralph Martin, acts as a litmus test to decide whether or not humans are on God's side. Either they give God praise or they withhold that acknowledgment and live only for themselves. So the phrase "Give glory to God!" in John 9:24 carries this meaning: "Admit the truth." It implies that when humans make a truthful confession of who they are, they cross over the threshold to a life of praise.[12]

At the root of all praise necessarily lies a spirit of wonderment. For a Christian, all forms of praise are given in some way to God, but the highest praise is immediately centered on God alone. Rudolf Otto's well-known description of God as *mysterium tremendum et fascinans*, "an awful yet alluring mystery," catches in a phrase the Augustinian God who incites thoughts and words of praise.[13] Praise originates in the self-abasing reverence for the Creator by a "minute part" of God's creation and is elicited by wonder-approaching amazement at the greatness of God. Augustine, in his role as teacher of praise (*doctor laudis*)[14] rightly observed that worship takes place by the offering of praise and thanksgiving.[15]

In summary, the character of God is a deciding factor in the evocation of our praise. The reasons for that praise are located in God's saving activity in human history. The biblical teaching invites us to praise in light of historical events that transpired independently of human engineering or forethought. Although God uses men and women as agents of God's redemptive purposes (e.g., Moses and the deliverance of the Hebrew people), it is nonetheless God's decision to act, and God always reserves the initiative. Thus, praise is directed to God, who works wonders sovereignly.[16] Moreover, Martin rightly notes that praise is not an exercise suspended on human feelings or governed by our emotional state alone. Even when worshipers are low in spirit, they are bidden to raise up their heads and contemplate the "mighty works of God" done "out there," whether or not they "feel" at that moment like celebrating God. And it is that recall and contemplation of what God once did that can be as cordial to their drooping spirits as the psalmist found when life's mysteries were too enigmatic and threatening for him.[17]

Not only are there different expressions of praise, but there are also different forms of praise. David F. Ford and Daniel W. Hardy, in *Living in Praise*, list at least four viable modes of praise: word-centered praise, sacramental praise, spontaneous praise, and silent praise.[18]

WORD-CENTERED PRAISE

In the Christian church word-centered praise is in line with the Jewish synagogue worship that had such a great influence on Christianity. This type of praise focuses on the contents of the Bible, on preaching to stir response to the "word of God," on prayer, and on psalms or hymns gathering all of this into praise. In the Catholic tradition one finds expressions of word-centered praise in the first part of the Eucharist and in the monastic offices. According to Ford and Hardy, the Reformation saw a great renewal of word-centered praise, especially in prophetic preaching. The aim of such preaching was above all to glorify God by proclaiming what God has done, with the response expressed supremely in lives of thanks and praise. Both singing and prayer were also instruments of word-centered praise.

SACRAMENTAL PRAISE

Sacramental praise in the narrower sense is centered in the Eucharist (or Lord's Supper, mass, breaking of bread, or Holy Communion). This form of praise originates in Jesus' last meal with his disciples before his death. It is viewed by many as the most distinctive Christian act of praise, for at the heart of this praise is the relationship of Jesus to his Father, which John sees as a mutual glorifying. According to Ford and Hardy, it is the explosive nuclear center whose spirit powers all praise, and at the center of this nucleus is the death and resurrection of Jesus. The Eucharist allows participation in this death and life in a sacramental way and imprints its pattern on all Christian praise.

> They remember a history, with the vital difference that the main character of this story is believed to be alive, present and communicating his life and words. And in all this the bonds between them are strengthened, in ways already suggested, with the praise of word and sacrament inextricably interwoven.[19]

SPONTANEOUS PRAISE

In the worship of the early church as reflected in the New Testament, it seems that at least in some of the congregations the celebration of the Lord's Supper, together with preaching, praise, and the use of Scripture, were all embraced in free charismatic worship. Worshipers would respond spontaneously to the stirring of the Holy Spirit, with various people speaking in tongues, teaching, and offering interpretations, prophecies, songs, and various other gifts. Everything pointed to a vigorous intensity of free praise in which all could participate.

The novelty of Christianity in relation to Judaism was not just its belief that Jesus was the Messiah but also its claim that the Holy Spirit, quenched for centuries, had been poured out again. It inspired fresh and spontaneous praise and proclamation, with evangelism as the horizontal dimension of praise—the content of praise repeated and explained to others so that they can join the community of praise. The Holy Spirit was for all Christians, so there was bound to be a transformation of worship as whole congregations reached a new level of free expression in praise and various gifts.[20]

SILENT PRAISE

There are many qualities and levels of silence. Silence can be 1) an act of humble waiting and adoration that lets God have God's way without hindrance; 2) the necessary prelude to right hearing or acting; 3) the best way to follow hearing, speaking, or acting; 4) the excess or overflow of speech into amazed love, delight, or conviction; 5) the form of freedom best suited to let everyone in a group worship at his or her own level; 6) a medium through which people are strongly bound to each other; or 7) the ultimate in spiritual realism before a God who is simply beyond all we can say or do.[21] Among Quakers and monastic traditions in both Eastern and Western Christianity there is a wealth of experience of silence before God and its climax in adoration. To the contemporary American worshiper silence may mean various things. For example, if there is a lull in worship where there is silence, it may be interpreted as a poorly organized program or as something gone wrong, but for a context-oriented group such as the Japanese, silence is of central importance, conveying respect and unity in their worship of God and harmony and empathy in their relations with one another in the body of Christ.²² The praise of God has many dimensions, all of which can interact in the explicit praise of the Christian community.

DOXOLOGICAL PRAISE

In the discussion of their celebration homiletic, the form of praise about which Mitchell and Thomas write may best be described as word-centered praise. Specifically, they write about doxological praise, which usually comes at the close of the black sermon. A theology of doxology begins with God as the one who is worthy to be praised. The word *doxology* is derived from the Greek word *doxa* or "glory" and is often defined as a declaration of praise for God. Of the more than thirty definitions given in encyclopedias, commentaries, and so forth, none are in complete agreement. Eric Werner argues that at least two elements form the criteria necessary for a doxology: the proclamation of God's praise and an affirmation of God's infinity in time.²³ Thus the doxology found at the conclusion of the Lord's Prayer: "For thine is the kingdom, and the power, and the glory forever and ever. Amen!"

Werner notes that up to the fourth century the texts of doxologies ranged widely from a genuine prayer to a short formula at the end of an epistle or from a real liturgical preamble to an interjected, informal confirmation of faith.²⁴ While there is nothing in their writing to suggest that they disagree with Werner's definition, both Mitchell and Thomas stress a different type of performative doxology—that is, a heightened emotional ending to the sermon. While it is true that an emotive type of celebratory praise has long been at the heart of black preaching, black preachers are not the only ones who are known for ending their sermons on a doxological note. Chrysostom, Augustine, Calvin, and others ended their sermons with an ascription of praise, though not necessarily an emotional one like many African American preachers do today.²⁵ And to do so, according to Geoffrey Wainwright, was no mere formality on their part:

> It indicated the intention of the sermon itself and its aim of bringing others also to the praise of God on account of what had been proclaimed in Scripture and sermon. For the sermon expounds the story of God's dealings with the world and invites hearers to maintain their identity among the people who enthrone God on their praises (cf. Ps. 22:3). It does so on the basis of the reading

of Scriptures which, themselves, peppered with outburst of praise, recall the nature and works of God as revealed to Israel and made known in Jesus Christ.[26]

There are indeed different types of doxological praise. Mitchell and Thomas focus too intently on the emotional celebratory doxology, and therein lies a major problem with their homiletic. While the celebratory ending that has come to typify much African American preaching is clearly a legitimate way to end a sermon, there are other equally valid ways to close a sermon effectively that often go unacknowledged in the black preaching experience. Those who buy into this very pronounced, exaggerated close perpetuate the belief that if one does not end a sermon in this way, God has not been rightly praised. This understanding of doxology negatively affects black preaching and often causes the preacher to focus too much attention on not only the closing of the sermon but also his or her *performance*. All too many preachers are inclined to gauge the success of their preaching on the intensity of the emotional celebratory close and the much-hoped-for participatory response of the people, seeming to forget that preaching is

> the exposition of the word of God as contained in the Scriptures in such a way as to bring home its saving and liberating truth to the hearers, enabling them to understand that truth in relation to the situation of their daily lives in the world which Christ came to redeem and which those who are in Christ are called to serve.[27]

I continue to believe that this overemphasis on the celebratory close does harm to sound, effective content in much of African American preaching. Mitchell's primary argument for this heightened celebratory close is that a sermon, like a symphony, should have an elevated doxological ending:

> Emotion (not *emotionalism*) is a very vital part of all human experience. . . . The artistic pattern of closing a symphony with a climactic crescendo is about intentionally raising levels of emotion. By whatever name and in whatever form, concluding emotion is fine art, a vital option for preaching also.[28]

With this claim he justifies his call for this emotional denouement to black sermons. While Mitchell is right that every sermon should have a fitting doxological ending, heightened rhetoric is not the only way to achieve it, and the presence of heightened rhetoric, in and of itself, is no guarantee that God has indeed been praised.

Hebrew scholar H. Yavin studied different kinds of doxologies in religious and nonreligious literature alike and notes that doxologies or declarations of praise were common in ancient hymns and prayers and were often found in their concluding works.[29] The most famous are probably those in the book of Psalms (for example, Ps. 41:14; 72:18–19; 89:53; 106:48; and 150 declare with some minor variations, "Blessed be the LORD, God of Israel, from everlasting to everlasting. Amen and Amen").[30] Turning to Mesopotamia, Yavin found in addition to hymnal doxologies an extensive doxology in the form of fifty names (attributes) of Marduk that climaxes the Enuma Elish, the Babylonian creation story that glorifies Babylon's chief god. According to Yavin, both the psalms and the Enuma Elish are liturgical poetry; they were probably written for cultic or religious occasions and were certainly recited then:

> Their doxological endings serve a double purpose which is both religious and poetic; they express the religious credo of the community, and they serve a poetic function in the structure of their texts—they provide closure either for one composition or, as in Psalms, for an entire section or "book."[31]

But Yavin also observes that Jewish scholarly religious works such as Bible commentaries often end with a doxology. These works often conclude with a variation on the formula "Finished and complete. Praise to God, the Creator of the world."[32] Such doxologies provide an appropriate form of closure in these nonliturgical works, for Mesopotamian scribes and medieval scholars, living in societies that did not distinguish between the religious and the secular, naturally perceived their writings as religious endeavors in some sense. At the very least, a sense of humility would move the writer to render homage to the power that made the writing of texts possible, such as the goddess of writing or the lord of the universe. On a grander level, says Yavin, the author considered his or her writing a religious act, undertaken for the greater glory of God. Yavin further notes that even modern biblical scholars who attempt to separate their scholarship from their religious beliefs include doxologies as endings more often than has been realized. Yavin considers the mention of the name of God or Jesus at the end of a work, or even a reference to religious beliefs, to be a form of doxology not unlike those that occur in ancient compositions. To judge from their endings, says Yavin, many modern works of biblical criticism continue to be written for the greater glory of God or, even more obvious to sensitive Jewish eyes, for the greater glory of the church. The point to be made is that a doxology detached from any notion of emotion can still be a valid doxology if it is indeed a declaration of praise for God.

What is also helpful for our current search for ways to engage in different kinds of doxological praise are the categories that Yavin establishes for closing out works in general, be they religious or nonliturgical. Before moving to the different types of doxological endings, Yavin looks at the endings of scholarly works in general, noting that consciously or unconsciously many authors aim for a sense of closure in their writing. He notes four common ways to close any piece of writing:

1. A work may simply stop when it has made its last point. For instance, a biblical commentary ends when the last verse has been explicated; a historical study ends with the last event discussed; or a composition or even a sermon could simply end when the last point has been made. Yavin refers to such an ending as one without closure.
2. The end sums up the main point or thesis of the book, sometimes returning to the point of departure or even forming an *inclusion* (placing similar material at the beginning and end of a section). Many writers and preachers summarize their works by referring to the main points or focus of the piece before ending.
3. The ending projects toward the future. This is a common way to conclude narratives because it forms a bridge between the time of the tale and the time of the telling. In fairy tales it is the "and they lived happily ever after" ending. In scholarly expositions the future projected toward may be either the future of scholarship or the future of the subject under discussion.
4. The ending is reflected in the language of closure, which tends to become elevated. This is the literary analogue of the *ritard* (a gradual slowing down of a piece of music) or crescendo (a gradual increase in the loudness of a piece) at the end of many musical compositions, and it may be similar to the linguistic changes that have been demonstrated in poem endings.[33] It is also the type of ending that is at the heart of Mitchell's understanding of the celebratory close in black preaching.

Yavin notes that all four endings, or a combination of them, are widespread in both biblical and nonbiblical works. It is especially the case in biblical studies that the line between heightened language and projection toward the future, on the one hand, and doxology, on the other, begins to blur. So what an author may have intended simply as a form of closure turns into doxology. Yavin then moves on to discuss four different types of doxological endings, which he characterizes as 1) christological endings, 2) ethical-moral endings, 3) endings that use God's name, and 4) the "best is last" endings.

Christological Endings

Christological endings may employ heightened rhetoric, quotation, and/or projection toward the future, but they are all patently christological or done in christological form.[34] It is indeed a fitting way to close out a sermon on a doxological note. In a homily titled "The Necessity of the Wilderness," based on Mark 1:1–13, I intentionally close the sermon on a christological-doxological note. I open the sermon by describing the importance of the wilderness to the first hearers of Mark's Gospel and call attention to the fact that in Mark's Gospel there is theology in topography and prophecy in geography:

> Thus it is not by accident but rather by design that Mark mentions the word *wilderness* four times in the first thirteen verses of his prologue. Why? What was the importance of the wilderness for Mark and his first hearers? Owing to their past travels and travails there developed among the Israelites a wilderness tradition where they came to view the wilderness not so much as a place but as a symbol. The wilderness came to symbolize a place of preparation and repentance. The Israelites understood it as the place where they made ready for the achievement of new goals in God—preparation, but also the place where they turned from their past sins and disobedience toward God—repentance. So the wilderness symbolizes the place where one gets ready for God and also the place where one gets right with God.[35]

I go on to note that the wilderness is a place of extremes where one stands between the adversaries of God and the agents of God. The wilderness is a place of both warning and promise, but it is also the place where decisions are made and questions are resolved. To close out the brief sermon I note that all who follow Christ will have their wilderness experience but that we do not go to it or through it alone; we have One who has promised to help us. The content of the doxological ending that I chose for this sermon is christological in tone and in intent. Separate and apart from any heightened intonation or elevation in my voice, the words themselves are offered as doxology:

> In your own season of Spirit-driven, wilderness wandering do not faint or grow weary for one has gone before you who is able to help you. He has been tested not just in the wilderness but even unto Calvary. Jesus Christ is not only the king of the world, the Lord of the faith, the head of the church, and the captain of our salvation. He is also the overseer of the overcomers. Thus in the throes of your wilderness experience you can ask him to help you. He indeed will comfort, strengthen, and keep you. He has promised to carry you through. Amen!

The doxological ending for this sermon has Jesus Christ as its aim and end. There are no examples of human striving in the wilderness. There are no tail-end anecdotes to bring home the gravity of our own wilderness experience. The doxological focus is clearly and simply on Jesus Christ. Owing to the context in which this sermon was first preached—Princeton Seminary's Miller Chapel—there was no deliberate elevation in my voice and no contrived emotion to get a hearing. All effort was made to keep the focus on the work of Jesus Christ. The words themselves are intended to give honor and glory to God. The lack of emotion did not take away from my desire to ascribe praise to Jesus Christ as I closed this sermon. Those of us who proclaim the gospel have to trust that effectual praise is not determined by the intensity of our emotions.

Another example of this type of christological ending would be a sermon that compared and contrasted the first and second Adam spoken of in the Scriptures, with the fallen Adam of Genesis being our first Adam and Christ, our second Adam. Black preachers will often use this oral formula as their celebratory close, many times with an elevated tone in their voices. But even in the absence of emotion, this doxology is still christological in nature, and its content is offered in praise to God. This particular oral formula highlights the redemptive work of Jesus Christ:

> The first Adam had us put out of the garden, but the second Adam took us in.
> The first Adam ruined us, but the second Adam restored us.

> The first Adam made us orphans, but the second Adam made us sons and daughters of God.
> The first Adam took away our peace, but the second Adam gave us a peace that passes all understanding.
> The first Adam broke us, but the second Adam made us whole again.
> The first Adam left us scarred and downcast, but the second Adam lifted us up and healed our hurting souls.
> Thanks be to God for Jesus Christ![36]

A doxological ending that focuses on Jesus Christ is a fitting way to end a sermon. Such a close does not always demand an elevated tone, stepped-up rhythmic pace, or some notable change in the cadence of one's voice. Simply by way of the content of what is proclaimed, it is a legitimate declaration of praise to Jesus Christ. When emotion is legitimately present we should let the Spirit have its way, but we should take great care not to assume that heightened emotional fervor will trigger and/or guarantee the presence of fervent praise.

But as is often the case, a christological ending can indeed have an elevated close. In a sermon titled "Why Bother?" based on Paul's preaching on Mars Hill (Acts 17:16–23), I highlighted the need for the faithful to continue our witness to God's work in the world even in the face of an unconcerned and at times uncaring world.[37] I closed the sermon on a doxological note of praise to Jesus Christ. I urged the congregation of ministers to continue to preach Jesus Christ even in the midst of the ever-increasing secularization going on in the United States. It was purposely structured as celebratory praise with elevated voice though the focus remained on Jesus Christ:

> But tell it we must, for there is power in the telling of that old, old story. Too often we want to be deep and profound in our telling, but I encourage seminarians just to get the basic story straight. For there is power, wonder-working power in the telling of that old Story of the crucified One; the story of a savior and his love.
> Tell them of Jesus Christ. Tell them that he was born in Bethlehem, brought up in Nazareth, baptized in the Jordan, tempted in the wilderness, preached in Galilee, was arrested in Gethsemane, tried in Caesar's court, died on Calvary's cross, and rose from Joseph's tomb. Tell it! Tell it when you are up, and tell it when you are down. Tell it when all is well, and tell it when all is hell. Tell it when you are well received, and tell it when you are absolutely not

believed. Tell it until sinners are justified. Tell it until hell is terrified. Tell it until Jesus is magnified. And tell it until God is satisfied.

There are those occasions when the doxological ending is intentionally a mixture of christological praise accompanied by elevated rhetorical speech more akin to the buildup of a symphony orchestra's close. Such endings are honored and celebrated in black preaching. The point to be made here is that the elevated doxological ending is not the only way to close a sermon.

Ethical-Moral Endings

Ethical-moral endings are not specifically christological, but they have religious or ethical overtones. They pronounce a declaration of faith in God or in the words of Jesus.[38] Claudette Copeland's sermon titled "Tamar's Torn Robe," based on 2 Sam. 13:1–20, is an example of this type of ethical-moral ending.[39] In this passage that depicts the troubles of King David in his own household, Absalom's beautiful sister Tamar is coveted by Amnon, her half-brother who rapes her. From that moment on he expresses hatred for the girl he had abused. Copeland takes the story of this abused young woman to address the plight of women today who suffer from unhealthy family situations that have a negative impact on a woman's physical, emotional, and spiritual health. She notes how women are negatively affected by a past they did not bargain for but assures them that God stands ready to help them undo the damage that has been done. In a deductive sermonic format Copeland lays out the moral framework for an abused woman's path to wholeness: 1) She reminds women of God's wholesome intentions for their lives; 2) warns them to beware of the collusion of some men in their hurt and pain; 3) draws a distinction between love and lust; 4) speaks of inherent dangers when a mother's voice is absent; and 5) identifies the cry and the consequence of a woman in pain.

As she prepares to close the sermon Copeland reminds the women that like David, they can count on God to hear their cries: "David declares it thus: 'Hear my cry, O God; attend unto my prayer. From the end of the earth will I cry unto thee, when my heart is overwhelmed; lead me to the rock [that] is higher than I'" [Ps. 61:1 KJV]. Copeland then moves to her ethical-moral doxological close by admonishing women to cry unto God for help and healing. Says Copeland, "This is the good news: that whosoever calls on the name of the Lord shall be delivered. This is the good news!" She then makes a declaration of faith about her unshakeable faith in God. It constitutes an ethical-moral doxology:

> Cry until a thousand poisoned rivers empty out. God is coming!
>
> Cry until the rage gives way. God is listening.
>
> Cry in prayer. God is about to restore.
>
> Cry in therapy. God is sending help.
>
> Cry at the altar. God will come with arms and a mighty embrace.
>
> Cry until the confrontation arises. God will walk with you into a fearful past.
>
> Cry until the truth makes you stronger than all your violators. Silence has protected the guilty too long.
>
> Cry until you know the ear of the Lord has inclined toward you.
>
> Cry out . . . there will be an answer. A healing answer. A restoring answer. An empowering answer. There will be someone to hear, someone to protect, someone to recover you of your affliction.

Copeland is clearly giving praise to God for God's power to deliver. But this is no happy text chosen for its celebrative potential. It is a text filled with pain, dysfunction, and family intrigue. People are hurt and wounded. There is no call here to engage in celebrative emotional rejoicing. Copeland closes with a statement of faith in the power of God to deliver women from the worst situations and to make them whole again: "God through Jesus Christ bids you to come! Pain is not your permanent address! Amen." Yet she ends this sermon with a moral-ethical doxology. She ends in praise of God! It is celebratory not in the sense of joy and revelry but as worshipful praise to a God who has promised never to leave us, not even in our worst moments of pain and abuse.

Endings That Use God's Name

In this type of doxological ending the author/preacher manages to work God's name or a substitute for it into the close of the sermon.[40] In a sermon titled "It Will Surely Come,"[41] I speak of a season of waiting that comes to all of us from time to time. I remind the congregation that Habakkuk has entered into such a season of waiting in his own life, but the promise of God in this passage is that the vision awaits its appointed time. When we wait for that which God has promised, it will surely come! I close the sermon with the repeated use of God's name to demonstrate who stands behind the promise of this vision that awaits its appointed time:

> Who is it that makes this promise of a vision that awaits its appointed time? Is it some armchair spectator? Some tangled-tongue theologian, or some myopic mystic? No! It's God the alpha and the omega; God who promises and cannot lie; God who stands above the flux and flow of human history; God who is the same yesterday, today, and forevermore. This God says it will surely come. When you wait for that which God has promised, it is not a lie upon which you have fixed your heart, it is not a vain hope that shall bear no fruit, but it is a promise that will surely come.

I give praise at the close of this sermon to the all-wise God who makes this promise of a vision that awaits its appointed time. The doxology with God as its focus is intended to encourage listeners to wait with hope and patience in the firm conviction that the God who promises in this Habakkuk passage will surely come. Emotion may well be present in some who hear this sermon, especially those who are waiting in hope and patience on the promises of God in their lives, but I do not see it as my place to toy with their emotions in the way I close out the sermon. Even for those who are waiting, my desire is to have the focus remain on the God who makes the promises.

"Best Is Last" Endings

The "best is last" type of doxology has to do with arranging for a particular religious view to end and therefore to climax the work. It purposely sounds a triumphant note and leaves no doubt that what is closest to the author's heart has been saved for last.[42] P. S. Wilkinson, a prominent African American pastor from my Texas childhood days, closes his sermon titled "Traveling toward the Sunrise"[43] with the promise of an eschatological arrival home. The sermon is based on passages from Num. 21:10–11 and Gen. 28:15 in which God promises Jacob and the Israelites that he will not leave them nor forsake them on their journey home. When Wilkinson preached this sermon, he was president of the American Baptist State Convention of Texas. He was preaching to a district association celebrating their centennial year. Wilkinson was an old-style whooper who closed most of his sermons on a celebratory shout, clearly indicating that he preferred the "best is last" doxology as a way to end his sermons. The centennial occasion, the texts selected for the occasion, and the long-awaited celebration for those who were present that night all came together for a powerful doxological close:

> Let's journey toward the sunrise.
> The Lord will be with you children.
> The road you are traveling leads sometimes through green pastures,
> sometimes besides still waters,
> sometimes through deep and dark valleys,
> sometimes through dark turns.
> But let us ask no questions concerning the road,
> for the road you travel is the road that leads home.
> Home, home, home is where Jesus is.
> Home is where the mists roll away.
> Home is where no storm clouds rise.
> Home is where you put your sword up and lay your warfare
>   garments down.
> Oh home (whooping) is filled with doors and palaces.
> Home is my father's house
> Home is where the prisoners rest together and they hear not the
>   voice of the oppressor.
> Home is where the servant is free from his master.
> Home (whooping) is where the wicked cease from troubling, yes
>   (whooping)
> and the weary shall be at rest.
> Well, travel on. Well, keep traveling.
> The way may get dark, but he said I'll be a lamp unto your feet
>   and a light unto your pathway. Are you going to keep
>   traveling? (whooping)
> Just keep traveling, children.

In the bygone era of a whooper like Wilkinson, one senses in his best-is-last celebratory close a sincerity and earnestness, an invitation to join in the worshipful praise of the God about whom he is preaching. A spirit of rejoicing filled the air as he proclaimed a word of hope and encouragment to the 100-year old association. Wilkinson was more participant than performer as he invited the congregation to join him in praise and thanksgiving to the almighty God. This "best is last" doxology is the way many African American preachers choose to close their sermons. It is also the type of celebratory close that those standing outside the tradition may well have in mind when they think about celebration in African American preaching. Yavin has rightly shown that this very prominent celebratory close is one among several ways to give praise to God as one prepares to close a sermon or any other piece of religious material. The level of emotional excitement generated at the close of the sermon should not be the lone determinant of the efficacy of our praise. Those African American ministers who choose not to end their sermons on a high strung "best is last" doxology should in no way feel that their declarations and/or ascriptions of praise are less effective or less sincere. It is God who is to be praised, and there are a number of ways to approach that praise as we have tried to demonstrate in the foregoing pages.

SUMMARY

The four types of doxological endings are not mutually exclusive. It is not unusual to find them in combinations. For instance, the use of God's name, which is doxological in itself, often occurs in christological or ethical-moral endings. Yavin notes that doxologies take different forms, but the same things happen in all of them: The author ceases speaking about the Bible and begins to speak like the Bible. The author becomes one with the subject.[44] What is important to note in these different forms of doxologies is that the style of closing that many black preachers find attractive, that is, the one that resembles the grand-symphony ending in a concert, is not the only way to have a fitting doxological close to a sermon. If we could just hear that and believe it, it would take so much pressure off black preachers to close their sermons with the elevated language of a strong rhetorical close.

Brian Blount, president and professor of New Testament at Union Presbyterian Seminary in Richmond, Virginia, closes out his sermon on resurrection titled "Rise!"[45] by appealing to the God who can and does make a difference in the lives of the listeners. Traditional black preachers who are accustomed to the elevated rhetorical style would consider Blount's style and delivery to be somewhat understated. All who are familiar with Blount's preaching will know that he seldom, if ever, engages in the elevated language of the "best is last" type of doxology. The question is, Does that make this African American scholar's preaching less authentic, less powerful, or less filled with praise? I would argue that during the many times I've heard Blount preach there has been no indication in his voice that he intended to engage in any kind of emotion-laden celebratory close, yet his ending in this sermon—"*Rise!*"—so typical of Blount's preaching, is filled with doxological praise. From Mark 5 he recounts the narrative of the raising of the daughter of Jairus. The church to whom Blount is preaching is celebrating the renovation of their physical plant. As Blount closes the sermon he assures them that there is more going on here than the mere renovation of their church buildings:

> So what Jesus said to that twelve-year-old girl, I say to this 196-year-old congregation: *Rise!* Rise not just through budget difficulties, cost overruns, construction issues, and differences of opinion about what should go here, what should be done there. Rise to the occasion that this occasion represents. . . . First Presbyterian can do whatever God wants and needs it to do. You can rise to the occasion and raise a building. Now, go rise to the occasion and raise your community. Raise the people struggling in it. Raise the opportunities for mission in this place and beyond. Raise the hopes of folks hopeless in your midst. Raise the vision of a people who, though they think differently, live faithfully together. Raise the vison of one church continuing to believe that as God has made a difference, a concrete difference in your lives, so also you can and you will make a difference in the lives of people in this city. . . . Take hold of Jesus' hand, keep believing, keep building. Your building project is not over. Your building project has just begun. What you have built here is a preview of what you can and will build out there. So, *rise!*[46]

Blount lifts the sights of the congregation beyond a mere building project to the higher purposes of God in the world. He reminds them that it is God at work in and through the congregation enabling them to see the larger redemptive purposes of God in their church, their community, and their world. He also wants them to see the power of the resurrection in their everyday lives. Blount argues that it is God who has made a concrete difference in their lives in order that they might make a concrete difference in the lives of the people in their city. His final words to them are in praise to God and the great work God desires to do among them. So Blount admonishes them to *rise!*

There is no indication in this published sermon that Blount is aiming for some emotional buildup at the end. What we do have from him is a clear, concise, yet creative exposition of Mark 5 that involves the resurrection of Jairus's daughter from the dead. Yet we can say that Blount ends on a doxological note when we remember Werner's definition of *doxology*: the proclamation of God's praise, coupled with an affirmation of God's infinity in time. In Blount's doxological ending he says,

> Raise the vision of one church continuing to believe that as God has made a difference in your lives, a concrete difference in your lives, so also you can and you will make a concrete difference in the lives of people in this city. . . . That is why you are here, in this sanctuary this morning, in this community for the decades gone and the decades to come.

Here we have from Blount a note of praise to God for what God has done and will do in the lives of this congregation. In Yavin's categories it would be a "use of God's name" doxological ending. Blount declares that it is God at work partnering in and through the members of First Presbyterian Church in Raleigh, North Carolina, to make creation whole again. The decades gone and decades to come to which Blount refers speak pointedly to God's infinity in time, and not simply to the finite lives of the people who hear him preach on this special occasion. Blount's sermon definitely qualifies as ending on a note of doxological praise. As is true of all praiseworthy doxologies, as he prepares to close out his sermon and leave the congregation with what is closest to his heart in this message, he stops preaching about the Bible and starts preaching like the Bible. He uses the imperative mood as he extols the congregation to "rise!" It is no longer Blount talking about what happened in the Bible with Jesus and Jairus's sick daughter; it is Blount talking about what happens to a people when they hear and receive the witness of Scripture contained in the Bible.

How impoverished the African American pulpit will be if we look askance at this type of preaching from an African American preacher/scholar of Blount's caliber simply because he does not conform to traditional understandings of a celebratory close. Blount is indeed celebratory, and he is celebratory in the best sense. His celebration is not mere joy and revelry born of festivity but a celebration that keeps the Word front and center and invites all who listen to engage in the worshipful praise of the God about whom Blount speaks. There is no indication of contrived rhetoric in Blount's writing or in Blount's voice when you hear him preach, yet the word of God is proclaimed with power and conviction. The saints are nourished and invited time and time again by Blount to rejoice and celebrate in what God has done.

The foregoing examples are all legitimate ways to end a sermon on a note of doxological praise—christological, ethical/moral, the use of God's name, or "the best is last" type of doxology. It is also the case that some sermons may end with a combination of these doxological endings. Without a doubt endings are significant, for as the preacher attempts to bring closure to the message, the ending represents the thought that the preacher wanted his or her audience to be left with. This last thought may grow organically out of the last topic discussed; it may serve as a summation; or it may be an appendage to the main discussion. But however it arises, it sounds a hopeful note, and for this reason is able to provide closure.[47] There is no doubt that many black sermons contain the rhetoric of strong closure—elevated language, quotation, projection toward the future, and so forth. Black preachers should never be ashamed of that or attempt to deny that dimension of our preaching tradition, but we must also remember that it is not the only way to engage in a celebratory close to our sermons. It is the heartfelt declaration of praise that is most important in our preaching, and as we have discussed above, that declaration can be made known in any number of legitimate ways. Those of us who preach in the black tradition would do well to relieve ourselves of this notion that there is only one way to engage in these acts of worshipful praise that come at the climax of many African American sermons.[48]

Conclusion

Even when one takes into consideration all of the possible misuses of celebration in contemporary African American preaching, Mitchell and Thomas have been right in seeking to remove the barriers that prevent a worshiping community from offering to God exuberant, unabashed praise and thanksgiving. Both scholars are well-intentioned, for they have rightly taken the high-church term *celebration* and taught it into the liturgical life of many African American churches. They have given the concept of celebration life and vibrancy as a meaningful part—expectation even—of the African American religious experience and particularly the preaching event. Though Mitchell and Thomas are liturgically well-intentioned, there is a theological deficiency in their homiletic, for with their limited definitions of *celebration* they have not gone far enough in drawing a clear distinction between festive revelry and celebratory praise.

First, I maintain that *celebration* from a theological perspective must in the first instance be defined as "ritual acts of worshipful praise." To get at this more precise definition, one must make a clear-cut distinction between *festivity* as cultural phenomena and *celebration* as religious ritual even though both words are closely related. *Festivity* can be defined as mere joy and revelry (cultural) while *celebration*, used in a religious context, should be defined as "the worshipful praise of God," which often includes joy and revelry.

Second, I argue that Mitchell and Thomas have turned their quasi-theological understanding of celebration into a "works-righteousness" function. They see functionality as the primary worth of celebration since they want to *use* it to teach (pedagogy). Mitchell says that people remember and do what they celebrate.[1] Thomas declares that celebration in the final stages of the sermon functions as the joyful and ecstatic reinforcement of the truth already taught and delivered in the main body of the sermon.[2] Both Mitchell and Thomas take this common term from the history of the church, lighten its load, and give it a lesser meaning. Thomas admits that his use of *celebration* to mean "climactic utterance" was first defined by Mitchell. Thomas then lifted celebration up as the genius of African American preaching.[3] But in order to be theologically correct, the emphasis in contemporary celebration must remain on praise and not pedagogy. That, I argue, is one of the enduring contributions of African American preaching: climactic sermonic celebration as praise (doxology) and not as function (pedagogy). It is Mitchell's and Thomas's functional emphasis on celebration that causes their homiletic to come up short because it lacks a sufficient theological grounding.[4]

Third, I argue that while Mitchell and Thomas are right to suggest that praise should act in tandem with action, the rhythm between the two is neither triggered nor provoked through the use of embellished rhetoric purposely structured to evoke an emotional response in the listeners. There is no guarantee that emotionally laden speech that leads to their kind of celebration (emotional rejoicing) is a necessary kick-start to action. Adoration and action are binary in nature and interact with each other on the basis of a right understanding of the work of the Spirit as it relates to service and praise.[5] Adoration and action are indeed something human beings give to God, but we can only give to God what we have first received from God. The Spirit, not embellished rhetoric, is the source of both adoration and action.[6]

Celebration has long been understood theologically to issue forth into worshipful praise that acknowledges God's greatness and power.[7] But celebration as mere pedagogy, prompted by evocative language, permits—even encourages—an undue rhetorical emphasis that at the end of the day promises more than it can deliver. On the other hand, celebration that has as its aim and end the worshipful praise of God serves as an ever-present corrective to the misuse of this much-cherished feature in the black religious experience. This is especially the case when those who participate in those celebratory moments recognize that our worshipful praise is a gift of the Spirit.[8] If our celebration does not have its origin in God and does not come to us as a gift of the Spirit, at its best it can be little more than revelry born of ancient understandings of festivity—described by some as "praise-lite."

All is not lost in Mitchell's and Thomas's homiletic, however; it needs redirection, not reinvention. The high point of their homiletic should not be a high-strung climactic closing of the sermon. That is much too narrow an understanding of celebratory praise. The emphasis should be on the exposition of the Word, which when properly heard and received leads to praise. A more heightened focus on exegesis, exposition, proclamation, and delivery with a de-emphasis on celebration as a rhetorical tool will point preachers in the right direction to what they ought to be emphasizing in their preparation—the Word that enlivens us to who we are and what we have been called to do. If our celebration in worship does not rise to praise offered to God, then of necessity it must be stamped "Return to sender; address unknown!"

Finally, our understanding of celebration should be much broader than the vocal and demonstrative praise that most often comes during the climax of the preached word. I want to be clear in what I am arguing: I'm not arguing for a "real" theology as opposed to embodied practice. I'm certainly not suggesting that the end of our preaching is worshipful acts of praise and nothing else. Praise plays a vital function in our worship, but it is not the catalyst that evokes memory and action. Praise results from our awareness of God's accommodation to us. It is God's Word rightly proclaimed and rightly received as gift from the Spirit that moves us to act in the world with love, devotion, and service. Praise results from our recognition of the gifts of God! Praise does not guarantee those gifts or make them happen. They are of God and God alone, and for those reasons God alone is worthy to be praised!

In the interest of full disclosure, I admit that I was raised in the preaching style of the elevated, rhetorical, doxological ending. It is an integral part of who I am as a preacher, and after forty years of Christian ministry, it is the style of closing with which I am most comfortable. But I also recognize that there are other legitimate ways to close out a sermon, so in different settings I've learned how to end the same sermon in different ways. Every preacher should have the freedom to preach in a manner most suited to his or her gifts and talents. This book is an effort to open the pulpits of African Americans and others to the multiple dimensions of praise. The corrective that is offered says that even if preachers do not engage in traditional styles of celebratory, doxological praise as outlined by Mitchell's and Thomas's homiletic, they can hold firmly to the conviction that they have in their own way engaged in the worshipful praise of God.

This book is not a call for the black church to become silent. May it never be that the joy and worshipful praise that have come to characterize the black religious experience be hushed in our places of worship. Speaking people must never be replaced by silent objects as is the case in some churches today. Neither cathedrals in all of their beauty nor crucifixes and altars should ever replace the joyful praise of black worship.

Communion tables with open Bibles on stands, empty crosses, chalices, and collection plates must never end up speaking more eloquently of God and salvation than the preachers in the pulpit and the people in the pews.[9] In every generation there needs to be a fresh appraisal before God of the church by the church and a sustained attempt to seek both reformation and renewal at all levels of her life, including the level of congregational worship.[10]

> Praise the LORD!
>   O give thanks to the LORD, for he is good;
>   for his steadfast love endures forever.
> Who can utter the mighty doings of the LORD,
>   or declare all his praise?
>
>   (Ps. 106:1–2)

APPENDIX: SERMONS

CLEOPHUS J. LARUE: "THE NECESSITY OF THE WILDERNESS"[1]

Mark 1:1–13

In Mark's Gospel there is theology in topography and prophecy in geography. Thus it is not by accident but rather by design that Mark mentions the word *wilderness* four times in the first thirteen verses of his prologue. Why? What was the importance of the wilderness for Mark and his first hearers?

Owing to their past travels and travails, there developed among the Israelites a wilderness tradition where they came to view the wilderness not so much as a place but as a symbol. The wilderness came to symbolize a place of preparation and repentance. The Israelites understood it as the place where they made ready for the achievement of new goals in God—preparation—but also the place where they turned from their past sins and disobedience towards God—repentance. So the wilderness symbolizes the place where one gets ready for God and also the place where one gets right with God.

Moreover, the Israelites viewed the wilderness as a necessary place even though they regarded it as the home of demons and the haunt of forces hostile to God. Though it conjured up images of barrenness and remoteness, chaos and ruin, fiery serpents and windswept terrain, it was regarded as a necessity, for time spent in the wilderness expelled all notions of self-sufficiency. The wilderness is the place where the people of God truly come to understand that they cannot make the journey by themselves. In the wilderness two conflicting realities are always present: danger and divine help. On the one hand, the wilderness is the place of danger that threatens our very existence. It is the place where we are made to feel that there is no purposeful end and that maybe things will not turn out as we had hoped. On the other hand, it is the place of divine help. It is the place that illuminates God's power and determination to help us. The ministry of Jesus in Mark's Gospel begins in the wilderness, for Mark would have us to know that the ministry of the only begotten of God shall be conducted and carried out in the midst of danger and divinity.

Take note also of what went on with Jesus in the wilderness. He was tempted. He did not go there to pump up his popularity, or to test his messianic mettle, or to find favor in folly. The Spirit did not casually lead him there. The Spirit drove him there. *Ekballei* has the force of propulsion. He went there at the insistence of the Spirit to be tested, and so must we. The wilderness is not a place for rest and relaxation. It is the place where decisions are made and questions are resolved. It is the place where we decide on voice and vocation—whose voice we shall heed and whose calling we shall follow. Life-altering decisions are made in the wilderness because calling involves conflict. Temptation is tied to vocation.

Let there be no doubt as to whom we shall meet in the wilderness. There are four figures involved with Jesus in Mark's wilderness scene. You have the Spirit and ministering angels on one side, and the devil and the wild beasts on the other. The contrast contains a warning and a promise. The warning is that you can expect to be tested by the adversaries of God, but the promise is that you can count on being ministered to by the agents of God.

Notice the way in which Mark situates the figures in this scene. The forces of God are on both ends. The Spirit drives Jesus into the wilderness, and the angels minister to him after the test. The devil and the wild beasts are in the middle. Through this positioning Mark seems to suggest that the same power that leads you into the wilderness is able to sustain you while you are there and minister to you when the battle is over. In your own season of wilderness wandering make sure that whatever leads you in can lead you out. Mark, unlike Matthew and Luke, does not provide us with the outcome of the temptation. New Testament professor Ulrich Mauser says that the whole Gospel is an explanation of how Jesus was tempted. One thing seems certain: Mark's refusal to tell us the outcome indicates that our own struggle is an ongoing one.

In your own season of Spirit-driven wilderness wandering do not faint or grow weary, for one has gone before you who is able to help you. He has been tested not just in the wilderness but also at Calvary. Jesus Christ is not only the king of the world, the Lord of the faith, the head of the church, and the captain of our salvation. He is also the overseer of the overcomers; thus in the throes of your wilderness experience you can ask him to help you. He indeed will comfort, strengthen, and keep you. He has promised to carry you through. Amen!

CLEOPHUS J. LARUE: "WHY BOTHER?"[2]

Acts 17:16–23

Splattered across the front doors of a trendy restaurant in Palo Alto, California, were these words: "This is a bad place for a diet!" That most visible, in-your-face warning suggested to me that there are certain places where some requests are out of order and certain times where some appeals are in poor taste. No matter how noble, how worthy, how life-giving they are in and of themselves, there are certain times and certain places where it is simply unseemly to speak of some things.

In like manner it appears to me that we could splatter across the pages of our text this morning a similar warning: "This is a bad place for the gospel." Whether one regards Acts as a bona fide historiography or simply a piece of well-crafted Hellenistic literature, the gospel in Athens comes off sounding like a bunch of misguided, out-of-place "hooey."

Athens had seen and heard it all. In Paul's day, this once great and proud city was still considered the cultural and intellectual capital of the Roman Empire. It was a city steeped in art, literature, and learning. Of long standing, it had its names and its heroes and thus was not easily impressed by the new or the now. It was the place where Socrates, Aristotle, and Plato had lived and taught. And still counted among its sacred places was the Academy of Plato, the Lyceum of Aristotle, the porch of Zeno the Stoic, and the garden of Epicurus.

The voices of her poets had been heard throughout the civilized world, and the hands of her artists had filled her streets and temples with images of the gods. It was said of Athens that while strolling her streets you were more likely to meet a god than you were a man or a woman. Her myriad buildings and works of art stood in silent testimony to her former glory and grandeur.

Even though Luke goes to great lengths to create for us this scene where Paul is standing face to face with the philosophers in their own town and on their own turf, the upstart Christian gospel still comes off as out of place. It just doesn't seem to fit in Athens. The gospel seems to be out of its league in Athens. Athens is a bad place for the gospel.

The gospel seems all the more misplaced when one considers how Paul got to Athens in the first place. Athens is a temporary stopover. He did not arrive there by way of some well-thought-out missionary plan, but he arrived through happenstance and rerouting born of necessity because the work God had called him to do had not gone well in other places; it had not gone as he had prayed or planned. He arrived in Athens not on a set schedule but on a wing and prayer trying to rearrange what unforeseen circumstance had wrought. He does not enter the city fresh and friendly but enters disheveled, unkempt, bedraggled, woebegone, battle-scarred, and road weary. And because he is already in a bad mood, he is immediately repulsed by what he sees. He does not see a city filled with beautiful works of art but rather a city full of idols.

Yes, he probably could have been in a better mood. And yes, he probably would have been better received had he feigned some initial aesthetical appreciation for the works of art he found in the home of Hellenism's literati and intelligentsia. But when you've been stoned in Lystra, jailed in Philippi, threatened in Thessalonica, and hounded out of Berea, it is understandable that you might not be in a sightseeing mood when your friends finally drop you on the outskirts of Athens.

May I say here parenthetically, brothers and sisters in the faith, that sometimes we do our best work under life's most austere and trying circumstances; we do our best work when life is hard and the load is heavy; our best work when life finds us in a situation where we would prefer not to be and hope not long to stay. Like Paul, when life finds you there, do not bemoan your plight but lift up your head and your heart and go forward with the work God has assigned you to do.

So Paul ends up in Athens not through some grand plan but through happenstance. Even in the face of the uncertainty, tension, and anxiety that crowd his existence he continues to press his case for the gospel of Jesus Christ. But his arguing and preaching are not well received in Athens. When the people of Athens first heard Paul speak they asked with some derision and not a little contempt, "What does this babbler want to say?" What does this seed picker, this one who picks up just enough of an argument to speak about it in a superficial manner, have to say? In Athens God's international gospel globe-trotter, our first theologian, and the greatest preacher this side of Jesus Christ comes off sounding like an outgunned pip-squeak taking on a fight he must surely know he cannot win.

Even when invited to address the Aeropagus court, his speech/sermon does not go well. After that powerful sermon about the unknown God, there were no mass conversions and no triumphalist claims of victory. The word Luke chose to describe the impact of Paul's preaching in Athens was not "all" or "many" but "some." Luke said "some" scoffed, others said we will hear you again, but "some" believed.

He's in hoity-toity Athens, he did not intend to be there; he is not in a good mood; he is not well received; his preaching is so-so. The question just jumps out at you—"Why bother? Why put yourself through this? These people are not interested in hearing the gospel. This is a bad place for the gospel. You are just spinning your wheels trying to get them to see life from God's point of view. Why don't you leave these highfalutin, know-it-all Athenians alone and go on to Corinth where you might be appreciated?"

But do not give up so quickly, for there is some good news in the Athens experience. Running like a thread throughout the Luke–Acts schema is the notion of a universal offer of salvation. It was begun by the Messiah, who preached good news to the poor and outcast of his day, and picked up by his prophetic successors. Thus in Acts the gospel is proclaimed to poor widows and proconsuls, to jailers and sailors, merchants and military officers, kings and philosophers. Even in unreceptive Athens the message is clear: The gospel is to be preached to all! Paul has to preach in undesirable places, under less than ideal circumstances, and so do we, because of God's universal offer of salvation.

The gospel is to be proclaimed to all even if only received by some. I sometimes worry that those who consider themselves most faithful in our day seem the least sure about the universal appeal of the gospel. I worry that those who consider themselves to be the lone inheritors of the Christian witness seem the most determined to turn this gospel to some truncated, privatized religious hope palatable only to the few and the feeble-minded.

The gospel is to be proclaimed to all. We can all make that proclamation when ministry finds us in Jerusalem on the day of Pentecost, where thousands of souls are added to the church, but the true challenge is to make it when ministry finds us on the hard streets of a disinterested Athens. Somebody's got to go to Athens where they look at you strange and dismiss you out of hand and where they laugh at you to your face and lie on you quick, fast, and in a hurry. Somebody has to speak the good news in a bad place.

This gospel is to be proclaimed to all. It has universal appeal and power. It's not up to us to enforce it or effect it. We are to tell it. The power is not in us but in God. Some of us act as if we do not trust the gospel to work its way through tough situations. But be it Athens or Jerusalem, the gospel is to be proclaimed to all.

That is what we are to do, tell the good news of what God has done for us in Jesus Christ, the good news of the coming reign of God, the good news of the power of the gospel to change and transform lives even in this twenty-first century. It is to be proclaimed to all, even if only received by some.

Granted, it's going to be more difficult to get a hearing in this day because we all live in a time of what Microsoft researcher Linda Stone calls CPA—continuous partial attention. Owing to modern technology we can answer e-mail, talk to the children, and hold a conversation on our cell phones at the same time with no one thing fully claiming our attention. (It will be more difficult to get a hearing now because very little fully claims our attention now.)

It will be more difficult now because a recent publication on the proliferation of fast food in America confirmed what many suspected all along: that the McDonald Golden Arches have now replaced the Christian cross as the more widely recognizable symbol in the world. "Just As I Am" has been replaced by "You deserve a break today." It will be more difficult now because of the many implications of the postmodern era, with its dismissal of metanarratives and its debunking of truth with a capital T.

But tell it we must, for there is power in the telling of that old, old story. Too often we want to be deep and profound in our telling, but I encourage seminarians just to get the basic story straight. For there is power, wonder-working power in the telling of that old story of the crucified One: the story of a savior and his love.

Tell them of Jesus Christ. Tell them that he was born in Bethlehem, brought up in Nazareth, baptized in the Jordan, tempted in the wilderness, preached in Galilee, was arrested in Gethsemane, tried in Caesar's court, died on Calvary's cross, and rose from Joseph's tomb. Tell it! Tell it when you are up, and tell it when you are down. Tell it when all is well, and tell it when all is hell. Tell it when you are well received, and tell it when you are absolutely not believed. Tell it until sinners are justified. Tell it until hell is terrified. Tell it until Jesus is magnified. And tell it until God is satisfied. Amen. So why bother? Because that is our commission and those are our orders.

PASCHAL SAMPSON WILKINSON SR.: "TRAVELING TOWARD THE SUNRISE"[3]

Numbers 21:10–11

The Lord has given me these words for a text, taken from Numbers, the twenty-first chapter, the tenth and parts of the eleventh verse. And it reads thus: "Andthe children of Israel . . . journeyed . . . in the wilderness . . . toward the sunrising" (KJV). Let's look at that again: "And the children of Israel journeyed in the wilderness toward the sunrise." Then the context is taken from Gen. 28:15 [KJV], which says, "Behold, I am with thee and will keep thee in all places wither thou goest, for I will not leave thee until I have done that which I have spoken to thee of." (KJV)

The Lord has given me these words for a subject tonight for the centennial occasion: Traveling toward the sunrise, traveling toward the sunrise. One hundred years old you are. How far back does an hundred years reach? You were thirty-four years old when I was born. You were forty-three years old when I met the Lord. You were forty-nine years old when I started preaching. How far back is a hundred years? I admit I'm slow now. If there's anybody here who has not heard me, I want to tell you, I'm slow. None of us here are a hundred years old. Well, these hundred years extends over smooth and rough road; it extends over valleys and hills; it is marked by winds and storms. It is marked by fair days and cloudy days. The American Baptist Western District's first hundred years has been marked by shouts of joy and tears of sorrow. It has been marked by baptisms and Lord's Suppers, and it has also been marked by life and by death. Tonight, in the battlements of heaven is another Western District delegation, witnessing from the upper deep in glory this centennial association. Some of them left young, some left in middle age, and some left as an old-timer. Some were moderators; some were pastors and evangelists, some deacons, some missionary workers, some choir members, some ushers. And some with no official title but a child of the king. But they look down upon us tonight. And don't you leave here tonight without you saying Amen. And if you're ashamed to say amen you wait until we dismiss, and then say it. This delegation from above wants to know, Are you satisfied with your hundred year's accomplishment? Are you going to sit back on your laurels? Or what will be your goal in the second century of your existence? I think I feel your spirit. Yea, I think I sense your emotions. Yea, I think you would say to them that you are traveling toward the sunrise. Many of the saints of God have found it an unspeakable blessing to look back upon the past and say, Look where the Lord has brought us. I'm going to try to be calm here tonight. None of us will be here in the second century celebration.

Traveling toward the sunrise. Takes us through various scenes and dangers. The children of Israel were journeying through an uninspiring land. Journeying through a wasted desert. Yea, an empty wilderness. But they were upheld by the hope of a glorious new day. Yea, they were upheld, by the hope of tomorrow morning, when night with its darkness and shadows would be left behind. They journeyed from Rameses Egypt, to Succoth and Etham. And then they went over to Migdol. They journeyed to Mara and over to Elam where they found twelve fountains of water and seventy palm trees. They left Edom and journeyed to the Red Sea. And then when they crossed the Red Sea, they journeyed to the Wilderness of Sin and encamped at Elish. They left Elish and journeyed to Rephidim, and from Rephidim they journeyed to the wilderness of Sinai. And from the wilderness of Sinai, they encamped at Hezaroth. And from Hezaroth to Mitmah, and then to Ezion Geber, and then they journeyed to the wilderness of Zin, which is Kadesh. And they journeyed from Kadesh to Mt. Hor and from Mt. Hor to Zalmoa. And then they departed over to Obeth, and they journeyed from Obeth to the border of Moab. And then they came to the Jordan, and they crossed the Jordan into the promised land.

Well, as I look around here, I see you've been journeying from St. Luke to Ebenezer, and Ebenezer to Mt. Pisgah and New Hope, and from New Hope to Progressive Second, and Union Baptist and West Tabernacle, and from West Tabernacle to Mt. Pilgrim and Mt. Zion, and from Mt. Zion to Rising Star, and Friendship, and New Light. And from New Light to Mt. Calvary, and from Mt. Calvary to Macedonia and Mt. Moriah. And from Mt. Moriah to St. John First Baptist, and from St. John First Baptist to Star of Zion and Antioch. From Antioch to True Faith, and from True Faith to Greater Zion, and you journeyed from Greater Zion to Bethlehem, and from Bethlehem to Mt. Olive and First Baptist, and you've journeyed from First Baptist to St. John in Galveston, and then back to Calvary First Baptist Church, and here you are at Mt. Salem.

Your travels to this centennial hour have been similar to that expressed by the Israelites, and you sing, "Through many dangers toils and snares we have already come. 'Twas grace, (yes) 'twas grace that brought us safe thus far and grace will lead us on." Yes, you are like Israel travelers whose hopes are fixed on what is before you and what is beyond. You are men and women of faith traveling to the end of the road. I used to pastor a dear old saint whose husband is here tonight. And she used to tell her covenant, and she used to always say, "Brother Pastor, I got to see what the end is going to be." So you are traveling toward the end. Yes, you are road makers presenting an example of courage and victory. You are men and women of vision, always looking ahead. And as you begin your second one hundred years traveling toward the sunrise, let us begin by filling the air with a song of rejoicing, for we are wayfarers traveling to a better land. I think I hear you saying, "Trials dark on every hand, and we cannot understand all the ways that God would lead us to that blessed promised land, but he'll guide us with his eye, and we'll follow 'till we die, and we'll understand it better bye and bye." (Yes)

You're traveling to a land where dawns are forgotten. You're traveling to a land where glory has its dwelling place. A land where life begins and where there is eternal springtime. But remember the Lord told me to tell you, "I am with thee." And I'm getting ready to quit now. I come to tell you tonight he will be with you to take your part. He will be with you to be on your side. He will be with you to hold you up. He will be with you to plead your cause. He told me to tell you, he'd be with you in all your joys and in all your sufferings to bring you out. He told me to tell you, brother preachers, he would be with you in the pulpit. He told me to tell you, brothers and sisters, that he would be with you in the pew. So travel on, for the Lord told me to tell you that he would be with you on Sabbath days and on week days; on fair days and on foul days. He would be with you on winter days and summer days. He'd be with you in your failures, and he'd be with you in your successes. Methinks I hear in the Spirit some Western District Saint who recognizes that he's traveling toward the sunrise, but not traveling alone. So I hear you saying, "Lord, I've started to walk in the light, shining upon me from heaven so bright, I bade the world and its follies adieu. Oh, I've started in Jesus and I'm going through." Then I think I hear you say, "I'd rather walk with Jesus alone, than have for my pillow like Jacob a stone, living each moment with his face in view than to shrink from my pathway and fail to go through."

Yes, are you going? Are you journeying? Let's journey toward the sunrise. The Lord will be with you, children. The road you are traveling leads sometime through green pastures, sometimes besides still waters, sometimes through deep and dark valleys, sometimes through dark turns. But let us ask no questions concerning the road, for the road you travel is the road that leads home. Home, home, home, is where Jesus is. Home is where the mists roll away. Home is where no storm clouds rise. Home is where you put your sword up and lay your warfare garments down. Oh, home (whooping) is filled with doors and palaces. Home is my father's house. Home is where the prisoners rest together and they hear not the voice of the oppressor. Home is where the servant is free from his master. Home (whooping) is where the wicked cease from troubling, yes (whooping) and the weary shall be at rest. Well, travel on. Well, keep traveling. The way may get dark, but he said, "I'll be a lamp unto your feet and a light unto your pathway." Are you going to keep traveling? (whooping)

Just keep traveling, children, the night may get dark, but he'll shine on your pathway. Let me close here tonight. Let me close here tonight with my own personal testimony. I'd like to tell you that as you travel, I'm on the road, too. Oh, I've been on the road fifty-seven years. Oh, oh, it's been dark, but I've been traveling. Oh, one of these mornings I'm going to be almost home and I'm going tell Raphael you tell Sinclair that I'm coming home. And then Sinclair is going to tell Gabriel that I'm coming home. Oh, oh, when I get home, yes. I'm going to go down to Abraham's mansion, and I'm going to talk with Abraham, and I'm going to ask him, "How did you feel when you said, 'The Lord will provide'? And then I'm going to leave Abraham; I'm going to go up to David's mansion, and I'm going to tell David, "Let me hear you play on your harp." And I can hear David play, "The Lord, Lord, the Lord, is my shepherd and I shall not want." And then David is going to lay his harp down, and I'm going to say, "Play a little more." And I can hear David play that he makes me to lie down in green pastures, and he leads me besides the still waters. And then David is going to lay his harp down, and I'm going to say, "Play a little more." And I'm going to hear him say, "He leads me in the paths of righteousness for his name's sake," and then lay his harp down, and I'm going to say, "Play a little more. Oh, I just got home, so play a little more. Oh, I've been traveling, so play a little more."

BRIAN K. BLOUNT:
"RISE!"[4]

Mark 5:21–24, 35–43

Why are you here? I know people ask a lot of rhetorical questions these days. Sometimes they know and you know the answer before they finish the question. Does this dress make me look fat? Sometimes they really don't expect an answer; they're just making conversation. Hot enough for you? Sometimes they're trying to make a point. Trying to slide it in without having to argue about it. Are you *really* going to wear that tie? Rhetorical questions don't expect real answers. But I do. My question does. *Why are you here? Why did you come?*

When Jesus walks into the gathering of folks mourning the death of Jairus's twelve-year-old daughter, I suspect most of them are cynically whispering that question under their breaths: Why did he come? *Why is he here?* "What can Jesus do for the dead?"

That question is intended to be rhetorical. They already know the answer: *Nothing*. There is absolutely nothing anyone of us, Jesus included, can do for the dead, except cry. Sure, Jesus has been operating at a level most people can hardly imagine. Healing the sick, curing the blind, undoing paralysis. It is hard enough to believe that someone can do *that!* This past summer, my family took some friends from New Jersey to Monticello, the home of Thomas Jefferson. We listened to a tour guide talk about Thomas Jefferson's Bible. Jefferson meticulously went through the Bible and cut out all of the miracle passages. In his Bible, where there used to be miracle stories, now there were just holes. Because you can believe some things about Jesus, but you cannot, if you're a modern, scientific man, believe in those miracles. Well, many people could not believe in miracles in the first century, when Jesus lived, either. That means that even before the girl died, when her parents were thinking about sending for Jesus, some of the onlookers, perhaps even the parents themselves, were already skeptical that Jesus could do anything meaningful at all to alter the impending tragedy of their situation.

I suspect that when the little girl's parents sent for Jesus, they were doing what some of us do when the lottery gets to be three hundred million dollars. We buy a ticket. Because, well, you never know . . . it could happen. The odds of winning the lottery, they say, are about the same as being hit by lightning while simultaneously being eaten by a shark. But we buy the ticket anyway, because, well, somebody's gotta win the thing! Take a chance. That's what a lottery is. Chance. That has to be what those little girl's parents were thinking. Chance. A lottery kind of chance.

But even they would have to admit that the chances of Jesus healing their daughter when she was so very sick were astronomical. The chance of him doing something to rectify her situation after she was dead? Worse than being hit by lightning while being eaten by a shark while getting hit on the little toe by a falling star while flying a spaceship while winning the lottery. There *are no* scenarios for that. You die, you're dead. End of story. End of you. Walking on water is unbelievable enough. Raising the dead? Well, there simply are no words to express the utter incredulity surrounding that.

So why are you here, Jesus? Why did you come? What is it that you think you are going to do?

We can excuse Jairus for playing this ludicrous life lottery. He is a dad. His little girl is dying. We are not surprised that before he surrenders, he exhausts every single option, even the crazy ones. We are also not surprised that, when he finds Jesus, he expects Jesus to respond positively to his plea. After all, Jairus is not an unimportant man. Mark describes him as a leader of the local synagogue. According to commentator Alan Culpepper, such a figure is "appointed to look after the synagogue and take care of the arrangements for the services there." Chosen from among the elders, his duties are to decide on matters such as who reads the Bible during the service and who leads the prayers. He is in charge of the building, if there is one, and ensures that nothing improper takes place within its bounds. Probably he is also wealthy. An ordinary person's house, if he is so fortunate as to have a house, consists of only one room for the entire family. But commentator Eugene Boring observes that, in this impoverished Palestinian world, Jairus's twelve-year-old daughter has her own room.

An important man like this, we are not surprised that he expects someone like Jesus to respond when he calls. Jesus? Well, Jesus surprises me. I am trying to figure out why he is here in this story, and just as soon as I think I understand, he confuses me. He is here, after all, to heal Jairus's dying daughter, right? So I am surprised when all of a sudden he stops going to Jairus's house in order to deal with a woman who just pops up out of nowhere, a nobody, with no name, whose condition is nowhere near as serious as the condition of Jairus's daughter.

I understand when an ambulance, hearing that the governor is having a heart attack, flips on its sirens and streaks out into traffic to get to the state house as fast as it can. I am confused when the ambulance turns off its siren, pulls over to the side of the road, and lets the paramedics get out to tend to some homeless woman who has fallen off her bike and maybe broken her leg. "Why," I want to ask the paramedics on the roadside, "are you *here*? To get into trouble?"

It does not seem to matter where Jesus is. The Gospel of Mark is only five chapters old by the time we come to this story about Jairus's daughter. But already, one thing is clear about Mark's principal character. Wherever Jesus is, he attracts trouble. Case in point: impurity, the kind of impurity that makes a holy person defiled and gets a holy person in trouble with the leaders of the holy people if he does not avoid contact with it. Lepers. Tax collectors. Sinners. Women. Especially out of nowhere, no name, nobody, bleeding woman. But Jesus? Impurity clings to him like lint. He cannot scrape the impurity or the people infested with impurity away from his person. So I am not surprised when, like a robe magnetized by static cling, Jesus draws a dramatically impure bleeding-for-twelve-years woman into direct touching contact. While Jesus is weaving his way through desperate human traffic, cutting off others with less dramatic ailments, so he can reach a dying girl in the nick of time, this woman detours him with her desperate, defiling touch. And instead of reading her the riot act and getting back in the fast lane to Jairus's house, Jesus praises her and then stops everything to have a conversation with her. A massive heart attack in the home of a wealthy, important leader of the people down the street, and the Jesus ambulance has pulled over to tend to this unnamed, unclean, unfortunate woman who has fallen off her bike. Why are you *here*, Jesus?

Maybe he is here to make the point that no one is, by virtue of office, title, stature, or financial value, worth more than even the humblest person in God's eyes. This no-named woman deserves Jesus' attention as much as Jairus does. Or maybe Jesus is here to make the point that God can do anything, overcome any obstacle. And though her chronic illness is nothing like the mortal illness stalking Jairus's daughter, it is clear that while no human doctor has been able to help her, Jesus can. Jesus does. *Without even trying!* Perhaps Mark is trying to make the point that for Jesus no human brokenness is irreversible. And maybe, just maybe, Jesus is *here* with this woman to make the point that his power to heal is a sign of an even greater power. Perhaps Jesus is feasting on these lesser troubles in order to demonstrate that he has the appetite for taking on the greatest of all human torments. Perhaps, like an athlete strengthening his body in the weight room in anticipation of the coming battle on the field, Jesus bulks up in the sick room by beating up on human disease in order to get ready for an all-out war with death.

I wonder whether there is an analogous reason as to why you are here this morning, celebrating the successful conclusion of this new building effort. There is, after all, so much desperation, destruction, and devastation in our world, happening like a heart attack all around us. One might rightly wonder why we pull off to the side of the road to celebrate the renovation of another building while so many lives are being torn asunder. But is what you are doing not somewhat analogous to what Jesus was doing? Is not this building update a part of your bulking up for the task ahead? Because renovating this space so wonderfully the way you have done so is not the real test. Just like Jesus' healing that woman with the twelve-year bleeding was not the real test. Yes, healing that woman was difficult. Yes, this building effort must have been difficult. Yes, her healing was necessary. Yes, if your ministry is to continue to thrive, this building effort was necessary. But rebuilding this building, restoring this property, is only the prelude to, the primer of, the preparation for the life-giving, life-renewing, life-restoring ministry that now will flow out of this building. Having bulked up your property, be sure now to use this property as a resource, as a catalyst for beating down the improprieties of death and deadly situations that wage war against God's people and God's causes. I believe that is why we are here this morning. Not only to celebrate the renewal of a building. But also to anticipate the power that this new building makes in you and for you possible.

As you *have* transformed broken brick and worn-out mortar, you *can* transform broken people and worn-out communities. As you *have* reshaped this entire block committing yourselves to the revitalization of the structure sitting atop it, you *can* reshape this entire city by committing yourselves to the revitalization of the people and the circumstances that are struggling in your midst. As you *have* reached deep into your pockets to generate the funds necessary to tear down the old structures and raise up this new edifice, you *can* reach deep inside your hearts and spirits and pockets to generate the vision necessary to tear down the old walls and older ways of divisive politics, lackluster mission, bland spirituality, and heartbroken lives that threaten God's people and raise up a loving, inclusive, passionate, spiritual way of being Presbyterian in Raleigh, North Carolina.

Oh, but there are some nonbelievers among us! Nonbelievers who do not believe that we have the kind of healing power it takes to engage successfully the death-dealing realities that daily destroy God's people. Sure, we can take dying infrastructure and raise up a new building, but there is no way we will ever be able to take some community's shattered vision, some person's eviscerated hope, . . . some little girl's dead corpse, and raise up new life. That is the way folks were thinking as they watched Jairus's daughter die. I suspect, having heard the hard news of his daughter's passing, it was how Jairus himself was thinking. Jesus knew it. This is why, after they tell Jairus, "Your daughter is dead," Jesus tells Jairus, "Do not fear, only believe."

The present tense of the Greek verb is very important just now. Jesus is not telling Jairus to *start* believing. He is telling Jairus to *keep* believing. Culpepper says it well: "The present imperative [believe] carries the sense of continuing action: Not a single act, but a steady attitude, of faith is called for. . . . The father has already shown faith by coming to Jesus—now he must go on believing." Jesus is telling him: "Jairus, don't stop now! Don't stop believing now! Jairus, you're just getting started with this believing thing. Don't just believe when it's easy, Jairus. Believe now that it's hard. Believe like you mean it, man!" But the stakes are so high now, the obstacles to believing in Jesus' power are so great now. Hard enough to believe in miracles. Impossible to believe that, once dead, a person can be brought back.

With the help of biblical scholars, we can imagine the scene taking place as Jesus and Jairus come to Jairus's home. Already, by now, the funeral for Jairus's daughter is underway. [Culpepper writes:] "In the ancient Mediterranean world, without embalming or refrigeration facilities, the dead were often buried on the day they died." At the funeral were, of course, Jairus's family, broken, no doubt, by grief. There was also the obligatory crowd of friends and acquaintances. As Culpepper puts it: "The father of an unmarried girl was responsible for her burial. 'Even the poorest in Israel should hire not less than two flutes and one wailing woman' (*m. Ketuboth* 4.4), but because of Jairus's status in the community, one can imagine a larger number of mourners."

Yes, you did hear correctly. Not only family and friends, but also professional mourners were hired for the funerals of important folks like Jairus. Usually women, these professional mourners would "weep and wail," stamp their feet, wring their hands, play the flute, beat on other instruments, and beat their chests. Today some larger churches are able to hire professional musicians and singers to help the volunteer church members amplify their sounds and voices. Imagine being a professional mourner, hired by a church to come and amplify the sound of weeping and mourning. Imagine trying to explain that job to someone. "Are you a member of First Presbyterian Church? I see you are going there a lot." "Oh, no, I'm not a member. I'm a mourner. They pay me to cry."

Yes, they did pay people to cry at funerals in first-century Palestine. But, . . . no in situations like the one surrounding Jairus's daughter, they did not have to pay anyone to laugh. Yet they are laughing at Jesus. Given the circumstances, laughter arose spontaneously, and perhaps appropriately. Given all that is going on around him, Jesus still thinks there is something he can do.

She is dead! Done. Discontinued. Definitive. And here comes this guy strolling in with the claim that he can make a difference. Admit it. If it happened today, amid all the deadness and all the grief, if someone strolled in the house and told the gathered family and friends, "I can fix this," you would have laughed, too. Not because it was funny. Because it was unbelievable that someone would have this kind of nerve at this kind of time. The questions would be flashing feverishly through your mind: Who *are* you? What do you think you are doing? Why are you here?

To demonstrate the full power of life over death. Death is not even really death, Jesus is ultimately claiming. Not the death we see and fear, anyway. And that is why he calls it "sleeping." She is not dead. She is asleep. As Boring makes clear, "Death is called 'sleep,' not to pretend it is not real, but to deny that it is ultimate." There is dead. And there is dead dead. Dead dead is when you are separated from God for all time, for eternity. That is the death to worry about. This death, this girl's death, the death we fret over day in and day out, this death is not ultimate. This death is akin to sleeping. From this death, there is a waking up. All of us will one day wake up from it. To make that case, to show it can and one day will be done for all of us, Jesus wakes up this little girl right now.

Stop being afraid of death, Jairus; it is only sleep, Jairus. Keep believing, in spite of death; keep living like you will rise beyond death and all the forces of doubt and betrayal and dissension and dispute and desperation that death inspires in the human spirit. If you live with this kind of belief, so that you are not even afraid of death, then you can and you will do anything. You can and you will rise beyond any obstacle, rise to any occasion.

I suspect that redoing and expanding this building required faith from you. As a church, you had to rise to this moment. You knew there was a chance this project could falter. Your capital campaign might fail to raise the required pledges. The economy might go bad, and people might not be able to fulfill their pledges. But the prospect of the project's dying did not deter you from doing what you wanted to do. Enacting the vision you wanted to enact. Making possible the ministry you want to make possible. Take that kind of believing, that kind of rising, into every aspect of your ministry, and you cannot only change this block: you can change this world.

No wonder, then, that when Jesus took that little girl's hand, he used the language of resurrection. The language that changes our understanding of our place in this world and in God's presence forever. The word he used was "Rise." "Little girl, rise" (Mark 5:41, my trans.). It is the word Mark used when, after her healing by Jesus, Peter's mother-in-law rose. It is the word Mark used when, after his healing by Jesus, the paralyzed man arose. It is the word Jesus used when he called forward a man with a withered hand by telling him to rise. It is the word the angel at the tomb used when he told the women that Jesus had been raised. That is why Jesus is there at that girl's bedside: to raise the specter of life in this atmosphere of death. He is as much there for us as he was for Jairus and his daughter. Jesus' words to Jairus are as much for us as they ever were for Jairus and his daughter. Even, perhaps especially, in the face of death, keep believing in life.

That is why Jesus is here with this dead little girl. It is why Jesus was not there at the empty tomb. By placing Jesus where God places Jesus in these critical, crucial moments, God is telling us to stop responding to death or deadly spiritual, personal, social, political, communal, or church situations by giving up. Respond by rising up. Let me show you how. Let me show you what is coming by what happen with Jesus. Jesus will rise. His resurrection is the promise of your own. His empty tomb is the promise that one day your tomb, too, will be empty. What Jesus does here by the bedside of Jairus's dead daughter is what movie studios do with their upcoming films: Jesus provides a trailer of a coming attraction, a preview of what his future and indeed our future will look like by resurrecting this little girl. She did rise! We shall rise!

Why is Jairus here? To keep believing. To provide an example of what it means, how much it takes, how much it means to keep believing.

Why is Jairus's daughter here? To rise, and in rising now to provide an assurance that all of us will one day rise beyond death, too.

Why is Jesus here? To demonstrate God's resurrection power.
Why are you here?

Sometimes I wonder, why am I here? I don't mean here in this pulpit. I know why I am *here*. You were gracious to invite me. And I am overjoyed to accept, particularly since I get to follow in a way the footsteps of Dr. Walter W. Moore, someone whom I consider a hero of the faith in the history of Union Presbyterian Seminary and the Presbyterian Church. I mean, sometimes I wonder, why am I here in this kind of ministry, the shepherding of theological education at Union? It is difficult to keep encouraged about the mainline church. It is difficult to keep encouraged about the circumstances surrounding my own seminary. Difficult financial situation. Hard to raise money in this environment, as you know. Sometimes I think about how much money I have to raise to realize the seminary's vision, and I break out into a sweat and just start laughing. Giggling out of control.

In those moments, sometimes, I start wishing I had gone into other more lucrative professions. Professions that will always be needed, even in down economies. People being people, people will always be getting into trouble. So we will always need lawyers. Some days, I wish I had been a lawyer. Humans being human, humans will always be getting physically broken or ill. So we will always need doctors. Some days, I wish I had been a doctor. People being outfitted with teeth so they can keep chewing their food will always want to be protecting their teeth so they keep chewing. So we will always need dentists. Some days, I wish I had been a dentist. People being wasteful, people will always be piling up trash. So we will always need sanitation engineers. Some days, I wish I had been a garbage collector. You know, they get to ride on those trucks and are out in the open, and they don't have anybody bothering them about budgets and fund-raising and theological disputes. There have been times when I have wished I was somewhere else doing something else.

I don't know so much about us, but I do think I know something about God. God will always call people into ministry. No matter what we Christians do to the church. No matter what we Christians do to each other. God will always call some Christians to lead the effort of sharing the good news of the resurrection of Jesus Christ and what his resurrection means for our resurrections. I want to be there for God and for the people God calls to help them build the curriculum and the facilities and the faculty that will equip them for the moment when God sends them into laughing, weeping crowds where death has taken over. That, in the end, is why I am here. Why are you here? Ask the question. Find the answer. Then act on that answer.

The answer will lie on the other side of difficulties. Perhaps not as difficult as a twelve-year bleeding, or the death of a little girl, but difficulties nonetheless. In those moments, the meaning of this passage is this: Keep believing. Keep moving. Rise! Don't rise above difficulties. Rise through them. Rise through the difficulties and so transform them into opportunities for new life, just as Jesus rose through the doubt and the laughter. Erased the doubt. Quieted the laughter. Transfigured the world.

So what Jesus said to Jairus, I say to you. Keep believing. Don't stop now! Now that you have finished this building, do not stop, you are just getting started. Do not just believe when you're fixing brick and lifting mortar; believe also when you are fixing vision and lifting people. Believe like you mean it, church! And then act like you believe. The way you have believed with this wonderful building project. Whatever difficulties arose—and I know there were some—you kept moving, you kept believing, you kept building. You rose through it all. So, what Jesus said to that twelve-year-old girl, I say to this 196-year-old congregation: *Rise.* Rise not just through budget difficulties, cost overruns, construction issues, and differences of opinion about what should go here, what should be done there. Rise to the occasion that this occasion represents. This occasion represents that when First Presbyterian puts its mind to it, First Presbyterian will put its resources behind it. And when First Presbyterian puts its mind to it and its resources behind it, First Presbyterian can do whatever God wants and needs it to do. You can rise to the occasion and raise a building. Now, go rise to the occasion and raise your community. Raise the people struggling in it. Raise the opportunities for mission in this place and beyond. Raise the hopes of folks hopeless in your midst. Raise the vision of a people who, though they think differently, live faithfully together. Raise the vision of one church continuing to believe that as God has made a difference, a concrete difference in your lives, so also you can and you will make a concrete difference in the lives of people in this city; believe that you will make a difference in the life of this city itself. Rise, First Presbyterian. Take hold of Jesus' hand, keep believing, keep building. Your building project is not over. Your building project has just begun. What you have built here is a preview of what you can and will build out there. So, *rise!* That is why you are here, in this sanctuary this morning, in this community for the decades gone and the decades to come. To celebrate. And . . . to rise.

CLAUDETTE ANDERSON COPELAND: "TAMAR'S TORN ROBE"[5]

2 Samuel 13:1–20

Christian life calls us to make decisions. But life sometime has already made some decisions for us. The issue of family life, and its impact upon a woman's physical, emotional, and spiritual health, is one of these areas. Sometimes decisions have already been made for us—by the time we arrive at adulthood, by the time we reach awareness, some things have already been set in motion. But the Christian life calls us, invites us, demands of us that we risk, look, examine, peek beneath the veil and make new decisions about our own redemption.

Persons are about as healthy as the families we come from. There is a spiritual dynamic in all of Scripture of "family blessing" and "family influences" and the streams that flow from "generation to generation." God knew the problems of first families, the problems of Adam and Eve, or the problems of your "mama and daddy." That is why we are invited into the family of God; why we need a new family, a spiritual rebirth, an opportunity to redeem, repair, refashion, and yes, reuse the issues of the natural family.

Family constellations hold family secrets. Family units contain emotional maps about who is connected to whom, in love, in anger, in violation, or in care.

The first family can bequeath to us good genes, a strong sense of self, integrity, and identity. The first family can set our sights toward the stars and give us models for living, road maps to our life mate, and the raw material for knitting together a soul. We will fight outsiders who say the things we *know are true* about our family insiders. ("Playing the dozens is dangerous.") Thank God, in so many ways for first families. But some of us can bear witness that a certain kind of "family past" can pollute a woman's present.

Family secrets can affect a woman's present sanity. Saved women. Spiritual women. Sanctified women. Scholarly women. But some women are affected by a past that we did not bargain for, and one we need the Lord to undo. And when we hear that voice, we must make radical decisions about facing our own desolation, letting go our own despair and deciding to change our minds, our ways, and our mourning garments.

The widespread epidemic of depression in churchgoing women, modern women, economically well-off, hardworking, educated women, can often be traced to the childhood devastations that have never been aired out.

The pollution of our emotional and, yes, physical health can sometimes be tied to the soul pollution that has never been healed. Our robes have been torn. Our beauty has been spoiled. Our souls have been bruised.

Jeremiah 8:11 echoes the reality of many church women: "You have healed the hurt of the daughter of my people slightly—superficially; dressed the wound of my people as though it was not serious." Preachers have paid attention to this "woman wound" to the point of our own comfort and convenience. We have shouted. We have sung songs. We have collected money and built buildings. We have offered programs and platforms. We have preached irrelevant sermons. And for their coming, Sunday after Sunday, women go away with "torn robes."

Sometimes for deep permanent healing we must probe beyond the persona, past the veneer of church pews, and look into the legacy of family life. And it will probably hurt. I invite you, today, to participate in your own redemption.

Let us consider the text: 2 Samuel 13 tells us several things.

There is first of all:

The Created Intention for the woman who is the tutor for our text. Tamar is a daughter of David; King David. She owns a position by relationship and by privilege. The paradigm. The original purpose. "God created them male and female, and gave THEM dominion, and blessed THEM...." Your present trouble will make you forget that you are loved and valued, and that God's created intention for every one of God's daughters, is good and very good. God intends women to live fully and well. To create. To share in riding upon the high places of the earth.

Second, we see the *Collusion of Men*:

The text opens with Amnon.... He is the oldest of David's sons; according to 1 Chronicles 3, he is born to David at Hebron, during the time of his first elevation as king. Ahinoam was his mother.

There is his third son Absalom, whose mother was a princess, Maacah, daughter of Talmai, king of Geshur. And at the end of the 1 Chronicles chapter, almost as an afterthought, almost in the margin of verse 9, it states, "and Tamar was their sister."

In the Samuel text is Jonadab the shrewd cousin, the instigator, who reminds Amnon of his male entitlement to get what he wants. There is David, the older father who should be wiser, who should be a protector, who should care. There is the personal servant at the door, complicit; consenting to Amnon's deed.

In society and in families, there is a certain kind of man in collusion with the destruction of our daughters. Not all men want to harm you, not all men are without honor or boundaries; not all men will fail to protect you or your children, abandon you emotionally or financially, or take advantage of your vulnerability. We love the brethren and desire their partnership. But there is a certain kind of man who must be exposed in our thinking. A certain kind of man that our daughters must be taught to recognize, and all that good, strong honorable men must speak truth to behind closed doors or in public platforms.

A certain kind of man who thinks it is his privilege to use women; who believes in his own entitlement simply because he is a male.

A certain kind of police officer, who refuses to take the domestic violence call seriously; a certain kind of judge who will never institute or reinforce the child support; a certain kind of professor who will barter with female students for grades or who will ignore the presence of female students because he believes they have trespassed by being there in his classroom. Trust me, there is a certain kind of preacher man who believes that women exist as property and as playmates, a certain kind of husband who is insulted by the notion that his wife is an equal human being to be loved; who has dreams and goals; who deserves to be talked to and honored.

In the text, there is a collusion among these men: a silent agreement; a mutual consent . . . not to interfere.

WE must remind our daughters to watch out for a certain kind of man (the man who won't meet your pastor, won't meet your parents, won't speak up to protect you; the man who will use marriage to you to mask his own lifestyle of sexual alternatives.) We must teach our sons not to yield to the pressure to be that certain kind of man in order to become acceptable in the clubs that validate a certain kind of manhood. God give them strength to avoid the collusion!

Third, there is the confusion between love and lust (v. 4).

How does this impact the health and wholeness of women? We are confused as women, because we learn secret confusions as little girls. One in three women will be forced into sexual activity in her lifetime by someone who is supposed to love her. Some statistics say that one in five men will at some point be sexually molested, fondled, or raped; probably by someone they thought they could trust: the priest, the coach, the scout leader, Mama's boyfriend who paraded as father.... Love gets confused with lust, and the violation is three to four times more likely to be a family member, friend, or someone who claimed to like you or love you than a stranger. And in 50 to 90 percent of the cases, it will remain a secret and go unreported.

When lust is confused with love early in life, women get saved, have their sins forgiven, love God, come to church, and get ready for heaven, but too often, they don't go on to be healed, healthy, or whole and get ready for life abundantly right down here.

Lust is a physical force, demanding to satisfy itself, at all costs.

Love is a spiritual force, determined to satisfy you at all cost.

Lust is a blinding force that consumes the reason, overrides the will, and silences the conscience. It makes one vexed, upset, agitated if it can't get its own way. Lust uses. Listen to the heart of Amnon. "It was hard to do anything to her. . . ." Lust manipulated. Lust lies.

Love, on the other hand, is health producing; it sacrifices its own immediate desire for your long-range good. Love protects; love provides; love does not keep score of wrongs; love does without so you can have . . . and never mentions it. Love is thou-centered, not I-centered. When lust is confused with love inside the family system we silence Tamar's voice; we keep her quiet in the brother's house; and she loves the guilty enough to protect them with her confused love.

Incest is soul pollution. Sexual violation is a vandalizing of the spirit. It tears up something.

"Tamar tore the richly ornamented robe, the kind that kings' daughters wore." Her created purpose is damaged. The collusion. The confusion.

Fourth, there is the *Convenience*—in the entire text, we have no "mother voice." There is opportunity for daughters to be spoiled when mothers are silent or absent from the daughters and sons in their own lives. The older brother requests, "Let Tamar come and dress the meat in my sight, as my sister." Some things, traditionally, a mother must do, in order for children to grow well. Mother is absent. Mother is busy. Contemporary mother is leaving our daughter's stuff in sight of the enemy. Are you that mother, who is consumed with your own agenda and of being cute, and in competition with your daughters? We cannot blame women for what men do, but we must remind each woman to do what we can do.

Be present for your daughters and your sons.

Be alert to see what you see.

Be vocal enough to tell the truth.

Be strong enough to cover, correct, counsel.

Be whole enough not to need a man at the expense of the safety of your children's need for you.

We must not make the spoiling of our children convenient to their enemy.

Finally, there is *the Cry and the Consequence*—Tamar is one of the few women in Scripture who have a voice: "I do not want this." "I do want honor." "Ask the king for me." But she is thrown away.... Amnon violates her; then the text says he hates her; discards her; despised her. And she internalizes the shame.

Guilt is what I am legitimately responsible for. When I am guilty I can take responsibility; repent and seek forgiveness; make retribution and hope for restoration. That is guilt. But shame is trickier. Shame is stickier.

Shame makes me become one with the event. Identifies me, engraves upon me, excludes me from the embrace of possibilities ever again. Shame makes me feel defective.... Shame makes me shrivel, and act out and try to be what I am not because I do not like what I am. Shame makes me eat, trying to fill a void that I can't touch. Shame makes me take chemicals to silence the accusing voices in my heart. Shame makes me attach to whomever comes along for the moment as a distraction from my own unspoken horror. This old shame makes my boundaries fuzzy, letting the wrong folks in and wandering into places I should not be, because I never learned to discern the difference. And worst of all, this old shame silences my voice and stops up my cry.

But this is the good news of the gospel! When I cry out, God stops in God's tracks! The eyes of the Lord run to and fro in the earth, looking for someone to be strong for. The broken-hearted, to bind up. The captive to set free. The prisoner to bring out of darkness. This is the good news: that whosoever calls upon the name of the Lord shall be delivered. This is the good news!

David declares it thus: "Hear my cry, O God; attend unto my prayer. From the end of the earth will I cry unto thee, when my heart is overwhelmed; lead me to the rock [that] is higher than I" (Ps. 61:1–2 KJV)." "This poor man cried, and the LORD heard [him], and saved him out of all his troubles" (Ps. 34:6 KJV).

Cry until a thousand poison rivers empty out. God is coming!
Cry until the rage gives way. God is listening.
Cry in prayer. God is about to restore.
Cry in therapy. God is sending help.
Cry at the altar. God will come with arms and a mighty embrace.
Cry until the confrontation arises. God will walk with you into a fearful past.
Cry until the truth makes you stronger than all your violators. Silence has protected the guilty too long.
Cry until you know the ear of the Lord has inclined toward you.
Cry out . . . there will be an answer. There will be someone to hear, someone to protect, someone to recover you of your affliction.

Do not miss the redemption when it comes. Tamar comes out! Damage has been done; we have been sinned against; some things have been torn. . . . But as Tamar, we can come out. She comes out of Absalom's house with her robe. Torn, but hers. The testimony of her survival.

Life can take many things. Some losses we did not deserve:

Poor parenting, betraying friends, financial reversals, dead children, dying marriages, failing health or faded dreams.

But every person is left with something . . . something with which to start again. Broken pieces, but start again!

Fragments of bread in the basket, but start again! A memory of how it was supposed to be, but start again!

She comes out with her robe. Torn, but a reminder that Satan did not get it all, that evil does not prevail ultimately, that there is a door of escape no matter how hard the trial. There is a past that she can trade in for a future. Redeemable.

Your life, my life, may be used; may have high mileage on it; may have sustained some accidents, and the frame may be bent. Men and women may judge us totally useless—"totaled." And relegate us to the junk pile of life.

But the spirit of the Lord is upon me to proclaim . . . grab your robe, hold it high, give voice to your testimony that the secrets are over! Put on the garment of praise; the truth sets you free!

Grab your torn-up robe. You are about to trade it in! Put on the garment of gladness.

Try the knob of Absalom's door; leave your despair.

God through Jesus Christ bids you to come! Pain is not your permanent address! Start walking! Amen.

CLEOPHUS J. LARUE: "IT WILL SURELY COME"[6]

Habakkuk 2:1–4

This self-sufficient age in which we live operates on the premise that we can always take charge of our lives. We are taught to believe that no matter what confronts us, with enough energy, courage, and fortitude, we can forge ahead and brush aside all obstacles and obstructions that impede our path.

This take-charge attitude is imparted to us as wisdom. It is instilled in us early on. It is the premise on which we are taught to succeed. This notion that we can always take charge of our lives is the reason, I believe, so many of us love to quote that portion of William Ernest Henley's "Invictus," which says,

> It matters not how strait the gate,
> How charged with punishments the scroll,
> I am the master of my fate;
> I am the captain of my soul.[7]

This sounds good, but the common understanding of it is not true, for it flies in the face of the providence of God. Too often, those who recite these lines glean from them some sense that they alone are responsible for the outcome of their lives. The psalmist in the long ago had a better sense of our destinies when he said, "Know ye that the LORD he is God. It is he that hath made us and not we ourselves. We are his people and the sheep of his pasture (Ps 100:3 KJV).

I suppose it is possible to think that we can always take charge of our lives, especially when we are young and healthy, or reasonably prosperous, or when we are completely in charge of our mental faculties. It is possible to believe life will always respond to our strong-willed wishes and desires, especially when rank and privilege are our constant companions and the bright morning of opportunity shines so radiantly upon our paths. Under such circumstances, one could conclude that this take-charge approach works in any and all situations.

But the truth of the matter is that different seasons come to all our lives. There are seasons when all that we touch turns to gold. There are seasons when the next step in our lives is so clear and so close we would seem foolish not to take it. There are those moments in life when God is in his heaven and all is right with the world. But such times do not last forever. In truth, seasons of loss, helplessness, and waiting come to all our lives.

One of life's most difficult lessons is learning how to wait on God through a dry and difficult season; a season where we are forced to wait, in spite of our nerves of steel and steadfast prayers, in spite of the American mind-set that tells us we can always take charge. We find ourselves unable to effect the kind of outcome we would like to see. It is for this reason—our difficulty in learning how to wait—that our text is taken from this strange, hard-to-find book called Habakkuk. This so-called minor prophet had a major word to say to us about how to wait on God.

In Habakkuk, we find a word of encouragement for those who have grown impatient waiting on the promises of God. We find a word of hope for those who, even now, are struggling to come to grips with dashed hopes, shattered dreams, and uncertain futures. There is a word for people who, because of life's uneven journey, find themselves ailing and, therefore, in need of a prescription for hard times. Habakkuk is just what the doctor ordered.

What is going on in the world of this seventh-century prophet that ushers in his own season of waiting? Habakkuk complains to God about the rampant injustice in Judean society. He asks God how long he would allow the oppression of the weak by the strong among God's own people, and he wondered how long it would be before God brought judgment upon God's own wayward people.

But Habakkuk did not like God's answer, for God told him he would use a heathen king and a heathen army—Nebuchadnezzar and the Babylonians—to discipline his own people. This answer confused Habakkuk. He knew that the Babylonians were no paragons of virtue, and he just could not believe that a pure and holy God would stand idly by and watch them swallow up his people.

Old Testament scholar J. J. M. Roberts says that it is at this point that Habakkuk, unwilling to accept God's answer, talks back to God—as did other great people of faith in the Old Testament. Difficult seasons will make you talk back to God, not out of irreverence but out of a sense of confusion and perplexity about the purposes of God in your life. It is easy to wait for God as long we can make some sense of what God is doing; as long as there is some discernible design to the movement of God in our lives. But when God shocks us and surprises us and refuses to answer our prayers as we said them, when we said them, and how we said them, then it becomes difficult to wait and hard not to talk back.

What do you do when you are no longer sure how God is going to work out God's purposes in your life? What do you do when you are not even sure that God is at work in your life? You are unhappy where you are and yet unsure about where God is leading. What do you do when you find yourself in a difficult season of waiting where heaven is silent or the trumpet is sounding forth an uncertain sound?

Our natural instinct, especially those of us who have bought into the take-charge attitude, is to try to make something happen; to try to make our season of waiting come to an end. It is here that T. S. Eliot's advice in "Ash Wednesday" is so appropriate: "Teach us to sit still."[8] There are seasons in all our lives when we shall have no choice but to wait.

Though we have no choice but to wait, we do have a choice as to how we shall wait. Some people wait out a difficult season in a spirit of rebellion. They go through life angry and disheartened, and they make their displeasure known to any and all who will listen. Some wait out a difficult season in a spirit of resignation. Life for them loses all perspective, so they become cynical about life, and they trudge forward with a dull and listless spirit. Of God's guiding hand and tender mercies they sarcastically proclaim, "*Que sera, sera*—What will be, will be."

There is, however, a third way to wait for God through our own dry and difficult seasons, and it is the wait of anticipation. Habakkuk suggests that this is the way the righteous wait. Their wait is alert and charged with expectation. Their stand is one of tip-toe anticipation. They wait in the fervent hope of a brighter tomorrow morning when night with all its shadows will be passed away.

Habakkuk, confused about the purposes of God in his life and the lives of his people, waits through a difficult season for an answer from God. Finally, God speaks to him of a vision whose fulfillment awaits its appointed time. An appointed time indicates a set time in the future that can neither be rushed nor delayed. An appointed time means God has a fixed and ordered time to move decisively in our lives. Its arrival and duration are ordered by God and not by us.

In the text before us, God does not even tell Habakkuk the contents of the vision. God simply assures him that it is a trustworthy vision that at the end shall speak and not lie. It is a vision in which Habakkuk can find security, for the one who reveals it is able to back up what he promises.

Who is it that makes this promise of a vision that awaits its appointed time? Is it some armchair spectator? Some tangled-tongue theologian, or some myopic mystic? No! It's God the alpha and the omega; God who promises and cannot lie; God who stands above the flux and flow of human history; God who is the same yesterday, today, and forevermore. This God says it will surely come. When you wait for that which God has promised, it is not a lie on which you have fixed your heart. It is not a vain hope that will bear no fruit. It is a promise that will surely come.

This is the word of hope I leave with you today. Dry and difficult seasons when we are forced to wait do not last forever. In their own way, they too are a part of the purposes of God. But when your season of waiting is over, what has been dry and desolate in your life shall blossom as a rose, and what has been so bitter to your soul shall be made sweet. Then, you, too, can join in singing that old African American spiritual:

> I'm so glad trouble don't last always
> O, my Lord, O, my Lord,
> What shall I do?

Notes

Introduction

1. *Christian Century Magazine* recently reported that 80 percent of people attending black Protestant congregations jump, shout, or dance during the main service, up from 66 percent in 1998. See *Christian Century* (October 15, 2014): 16.

2. According to the latest data from the Pew Research Center, the United States is a significantly less Christian country than it was several years ago. Although black Protestant church numbers have held steady at nearly 16 million, every tradition took a hit in the West as the numbers of people who claim no religious affiliation continues to climb. What is equally true in U.S. black religious denominations is that each successive age group is less connected than the group's parents. While nearly 86 percent of Americans say they grew up as Christians, nearly one in five say they aren't Christian anymore. See Cathy Lynn Grossman, "Religion in Decline, Nones on the Rise," *Christian Century* (June 2015): 12–13.

3. Ross Douthat, *Bad Religion: How We Became a Nation of Heretics* (New York: Free Press, 2012), 192–97.

4. This unquenchable consumerist desire found in black preachers and congregants alike was recently on display at one of the most distinguished black preaching conferences in America. A local car dealer was allowed to place Rolls-Royces, Mercedes-Benzs, and Cadillacs at the entrance of the auditorium. True to form, each day when entering the conference, one could see and hear people oohing and gasping over their desire to own one of these high-priced luxury vehicles.

5. Neil Postman, *Amusing Ourselves to Death: Public Discourse in the Age of Show Business* (New York: Penguin Books, 1985), 27–28.

6. *Amos 'n' Andy* was a radio and television sitcom that was popular from the 1920s through the 1950s. It often included crude and denigrating dialogue about black life in America's cities.

7. The sing-song chant that black ministers engage in while preaching.

8. Robert E. Webber, *Worship Is a Verb* (Nashville: Abbot Martyn, 1992), 23.

9. While we often talk of income inequality between whites and blacks, there is an ever-widening gap between the incomes of well-to-do blacks and their less fortunate brothers and sisters. And though many continue to worship in the same church, the haves, the wannabes, and the have-nots are being drawn into sharper distinctions in our churches. Also, see Michelle Alexander, *The New Jim*

Crow: Mass Incarceration in the Age of Colorblindness (New York: The New Press, 2012), 56.

10. Martin Luther King Jr., cited in Taylor Branch, *Parting the Waters: America in the King Years 1954–63* (New York: Simon & Schuster, 1988), 695–96.

11. Eddie Glaude, "The Black Church Is Dead," Feb. 24, 2010, http://huffingtonpost.com/eddie-glaude-jr-phd/the-black-church-is-dead_b_473815.html.

Chapter 1: The Celebratory Impulse in Black Preaching

1. Henry H. Mitchell, *Celebration and Experience in Preaching* (Nashville: Abingdon Press, 1990; rev. ed. 2008); and Frank A. Thomas, *They Like to Never Quit Praisin' God*, rev. ed. (Cleveland: Pilgrim Press, 2013; Cleveland: United Church Press, 1997). A recent addition to the published works on celebration is Luke Powery's *Spirit Speech: Lament and Celebration in Preaching* (Nashville: Abingdon Press, 2009). Powery wants to broaden Mitchell's understanding of celebration by pairing lament to celebration as another faithful response of worship to God. He argues that the Holy Spirit manifests itself through lament as well as celebration in preaching. Powery does not, however, challenge Mitchell's basic theological premise concerning celebration.

2. Henry H. Mitchell, *Black Preaching* (San Francisco: Harper & Row, 1970); *The Recovery of Preaching* (San Francisco: Harper & Row, 1977); and *Celebration and Experience* (1990). For the advancement of Mitchell's thinking on celebration see Thomas, *They Like to Never*, 181.

3. Harvey Cox, *The Feast of Fools: A Theological Essay on Festivity and Fantasy*. (New York: Harper & Row, 1969).

4. Ibid., 25.

5. Mitchell, *Black Preaching*, 40. Mitchell makes a passing reference here to Cox's work when he makes an argument for the validity of black cultural identity, but he does not address himself to Cox's primary thesis of festivity and fantasy, of which celebration is a vital component. In chap. 2 of *The Recovery of Preaching*, Mitchell outlines the various functions of celebration in black preaching.

6. James Earl Massey, *The Responsible Pulpit* (Anderson, IN: Warner, 1974), 110–11. The five types of African American preaching listed by Massey are labeled *functional, festive, communal, radical,* and *climactic.*

7. Ibid., 102–03. Massey, unlike Mitchell, actually cites Cox's three-pronged definition of *festivity* as (1) calculated excess, (2) celebrative affirmation—either "because of" or "in spite of"—and (3) juxtapositional contrast between the event and the everyday experience. Unfortunately, Massey chose not to pursue this line of inquiry even further in the early 1970s. It is also important to note that both Cox's and Massey's description of celebration contain some understanding of celebration as the praise of God as its ultimate end.

8. Thomas, *They Like to Never*, 18.

9. Thomas H. Troeger and Leonora Tubbs Tisdale, *A Sermon Workbook: Exercises in the Art and Craft of Preaching* (Nashville: Abingdon Press, 2013), 157–60. Troeger and Tisdale devote a section of their book to the contribution celebration has made to all preaching traditions. Mitchell himself took another look at celebration's contribution to preaching twenty years after the publication of *Celebration and Experience in Preaching*. See Henry Mitchell, "Celebration Renewed," in Wesley O. Allen, ed., *The Renewed Homiletic* (Minneapolis: Fortress Press, 2010), 63–80.

10. Timothy A. Lenchak, "Praise," in *The Collegeville Pastoral Dictionary of Biblical Theology*, ed. Carroll Stuhlmueller (Collegeville, MN: Liturgical Press, 1996), 752–54.

11. Geoffrey Wainwright, "The Praise of God in the Theological Reflection of the Church," *Interpretation* 9, no. 1 (Jan. 1985): 38.

12. Lenchak, "Praise," 752.

13. Pamela Ann Moeller, *Calvin's Doxology: Worship in the 1559 Institutes with a View to Contemporary Worship Renewal* (Allison Park, PA: Pickwick Publications, 1997), 55.

14. Saint Augustine, *On Christian Doctrine* (New York: Macmillan Publishing Co., 1958), 122.

15. Robert Smith Jr., *Doctrine That Dances: Bringing Doctrinal Preaching and Teaching to Life* (Nashville: B&H Academic, 2008), 107.

16. Cox, *Feast of Fools*, 48–55. The Hebrew Scriptures are full of references to "dancing before the Lord." Dance held a place of primacy in early Christian worship. Even when other traditions turned away from dance because of its explicitly sexual dimensions, the rhythmic movement and sensuality of swaying bodies never disappeared from black congregations and especially Pentecostal churches. In the eyes of many black congregants the sensuousness of the dance did not make it an unfit vehicle for the praise of God. See also Estrelda Y. Alexander, *Black Fire Reader: A Documentary Resource on African American Pentecostalism* (Eugene, OR: Cascade Books, 2013), 9–10.

17. William J. Woodruff, "Celebrate, Celebration," in *Baker's Evangelical Dictionary of Biblical Theology*, ed. Walter A. Elwell (Grand Rapids: Baker Books, 1996). "Celebrate" is the translation of the Hebrew verb *hagag*, which means to prepare, keep, or observe a feast or festival, from the noun *hag*, which indicates a feast or festival, and the verb *asaa*, which means to make or celebrate.

18. Lenchak, "Praise," 753.

Chapter 2: A Review of Henry Mitchell's and Frank Thomas's Celebration Homiletic

1. Henry Mitchell, *Celebration and Experience in Preaching* (Nashville: Abingdon Press, 1990), 7; hereafter referred to as *Celebration* (1990). I cite the first edition of Mitchell's book here because he makes no new argument for celebration in the revised edition that appeared in 2008. In his revised edition Mitchell said

of the 1990 publication, "Some of the basic ideas in *Celebration* have ceased to need prominent placement here, because they tend now to be taken for granted" (*Celebration and Experience in Preaching*, rev. ed. [Nashville: Abingdon Press, 2008], 7 ; hereafter cited as [*Celebration,* 2008]). He makes a more thorough argument for his understanding of celebration in the first edition.

2. *Celebration* (1990), 17.
3. Ibid., 18.
4. Ibid., 19.
5. Ibid., 19–20.
6. Ibid., 21.
7. Ibid., 22.
8. Ibid., 24.
9. Ibid., 25.
10. Ibid., 29.
11. Ibid.
12. Ibid., 26.
13. Ibid., 29.
14. Ibid., 30. In later writings, to his credit, Mitchell backs away from a totally functional approach, saying, "Whereas European American homiletics had primarily focused on the cognitive consciousness of the hearer, in this folk-generated method I emphasized intuitive consciousness as the sector of interactive human consciousness where faith and trust are retained. Additionally, I claimed that human emotions operate parallel to the intuitive, in another interacting sector of consciousness. Neither, however, was held to be the *source* of faith and trust. Faith and trust are gifts bestowed by the Holy Spirit." Though Mitchell has more clearly defined how celebration functions in his homiletic, he has not renounced his earlier understanding of the functional approach of his celebratory praise. See Henry Mitchell, "Celebration Renewed," in O. Wesley Allen, Jr., ed. *The Renewed Homiletic* (Minneapolis: Fortress Press, 2010), 64.

15. Mitchell, *Celebration*, 30.
16. Ibid., 31.
17. Ibid., 61. In the revised edition of *Celebration* Mitchell argues this same point saying, "There is a sense in which a sermon is a work of art, in parallel with great drama and symphonies. . . . Symphonies join sermons and dramatic plays in glorious, celebrative conclusions" (*Celebration* [2008], 32–33),
18. Mitchell, *Celebration*, 63. Mitchell holds to this belief in his revised volume but puts it into different words: "People recall best those things about which the associated emotional response was celebrative joy, along with being focused and *purposeful*" (Mitchell, *Celebration* [2008]), 35.
19. Mitchell, *Celebration*, 61.
20. Ibid., 63–64.
21. Ibid., 32.
22. Ibid., 34.

23. Frank A. Thomas, *They Like to Never Quit Praisin' God*, rev. ed. (Cleveland: Pilgrim Press, 2013), 17.
24. Ibid., 18.
25. Ibid.
26. Ibid., 20.
27. Ibid., 49.
28. Ibid.
29. Ibid.
30. Ibid., 22–28.
31. Ibid., 107–09.
32. Ibid., 113.
33. Ibid., 85–102.
34. Ibid., 102.
35. Ibid.
36. Ibid., 108.
37. Ibid., 49.

Chapter 3: The Problem with Celebration as an Evocative Rhetorical tool

1. Ian Pitt-Watson, *Preaching: A Kind of Folly* (Philadelphia: Westminster Press, 1976), 36. In preaching, Pitt-Watson claims it is primarily the will rather than the intellect or the emotions that the preacher is trying to involve. It is only after the will has been engaged that emotional involvement should follow.
2. John M. Quinn, *Praise in St. Augustine: Readings and Reflections* (Norwell, MA: Christopher Publishing House, 1987), vii.
3. See "Henry Mitchell: Narrative in the Black Tradition," in *A New Hearing: Living Options in Homiletic Method*, ed. Richard L. Eslinger (Nashville: Abingdon Press, 1987), 39–56; and see Mitchell, "Celebration Renewed," in O Wesley Allen, ed., *The Renewed Homiletic* (Minneapolis: Fortress Press, 2010), 64.
4. Henry Mitchell, *Celebration and Experience in Preaching* (Nashville: Abingdon Press, 1990), 26.
5. Don Saliers, *Worship as Theology: A Foretaste of Glory Divine* (Nashville: Abingdon Press, 1994), 24.
6. Pitt-Watson, *Preaching*, 36.
7. Marvin McMickle, "Effectiveness in Preaching: A Study of the Preferences in Sermons and the Influence of Sermons upon a Black Baptist Congregation," DMin project (Princeton, NJ: Princeton Theological Seminary, 1983), 37.
8. Frank A. Thomas, *They Like to Never Quit Praisin' God*, rev. ed. (Cleveland: Pilgrim Press, 2013), 108.
9. Henry Mitchell, *Celebration and Experience in Preaching*, rev. ed. (Nashville: Abingdon Press, 2008), 37; hereafter referred to as *Celebration* (2008). Thomas, *They Like to Never*, 108–9.

10. Mitchell, *Celebration* (1990), 67.

11. Cited in Thomas, *They Like to Never,* 100.

12. Wyatt Tee Walker, *The Soul of Black Worship* (New York: Martin Luther King Fellows Press, 1984), 14–19. Walker divides characteristics of black preaching into two categories: substantive and superficial. By substantive he means the content of black preaching, and by superficial he means the mode or form of black preaching. See ibid., 13.

13. Thomas, *They Like to Never,* ix–x. Mitchell and Thomas offer a few examples in their books where they are preaching before predominantly white audiences, but they provide no examples of white preachers whose sermons are structured in a way that lead to the type of celebratory close they are advocating.

14. Pamela Ann Moeller, *Calvin's Doxology: Worship in the 1559 Institutes with a View to Contemporary Worship Renewal* (Allison Park, PA: Pickwick Publications, 1997), 56. Calvin argues that the church is the normative environment for our coming to be in relationship with God. God has entrusted the church with the preaching of the gospel, the encounter with Christ, the forgiveness of sins, the whole ministry of the word, and the sacraments; these allow for and nurture our participation in the only real life, which is life in God.

15. See Albert Raboteau, "The Chanted Sermon" in *A Fire in the Bones: Reflections on African American Religious History* (Boston: Beacon Press, 1995), 141–51.

16. See McMickle, "Effectiveness in Preaching," where he reports that his congregation did not expect such oratorical heights each and every Sunday. Also see Raboteau's comments on whooping in "The Chanted Sermon."

17. The Reverend E. Dewey Smith, senior pastor/teacher of the House of Hope in Atlanta and the House of Hope, Macon, is a prime example of the reenergized "neo-whooper," who, though formally trained, chooses to maintain this art form in the closing of his sermons.

18. In the past it was assumed that the more educated a preacher became, the less inclined he or she would be to engage in the celebratory whooping style—a style believed to be more fitting for the spiritual preacher who was typically less well educated. However, any number of well-trained and highly effective younger ministers have chosen either to maintain or revive the whooping style in their sermons; thus I refer to them as "neo-whoopers."

19. Thomas, *They Like to Never,* 107.

20. Though the evidence is anecdotal at this point, any number of recent seminary graduates are leaving traditional black churches that prize the celebratory preaching style for churches in predominantly white denominations that are content to hear a substantive sermon without the hoopla of the traditional celebratory close. Among those denominations benefitting from this movement are United Methodists, United Churches of Christ, Episcopalians, and Presbyterians.

21. Dillard is cited in Saliers, *Worship as Theology,* 21.

22. Charles Rice, *The Embodied Word: Preaching as Art and Liturgy* (Minneapolis: Fortress Press, 1992), 22.

23. Cited in Adam L. Bond, *The Imposing Preacher: Samuel DeWitt Proctor and Black Public Faith* (Minneapolis: Fortress Press, 2013), 159.

24. Preaching that is devoid of lament has not always affected the black church in the way that it does today. One need only recall Harvey Cox's comments about celebration and the marginalized in *Feast of Fools*—"It is clear that the ability to celebrate with real abandon is most often found among people who are no strangers to pain and oppression" (Harvey Cox, *The Feast of Fools: A Theological Essay on Festivity and Fantasy* [New York: Harper & Row, 1969], 25).

25. Otis Moss III, *Blue Note Preaching in a Post-Soul World* (Louisville, KY: Westminster John Knox Press, 2015), 4.

26. Barbara A. Holmes, *Joy Unspeakable: Contemplative Practices of the Black Church* (Minneapolis: Fortress Press, 2004), 95.

27. Douglas John Hall, *Thinking the Faith: Christian Theology in a North American Context* (Minneapolis: Fortress Press, 1989), 33.

28. Hughes Oliphant Old, *Themes and Variations for a Christian Doxology* (Grand Rapids: Wm. B. Eerdmans Publishing Co., 1992), 20.

29. Luke Powery, *Spirit Speech: Lament and Celebration in Preaching* (Nashville: Abingdon Press, 2009), 35; Old, *Themes and Variations*, 20.

30. Sally Brown and Patrick Miller, eds., *Lament: Reclaiming Practices in Pulpit, Pew, and Public Square* (Louisville, KY: Westminster John Knox Press, 2005), 28.

31. Cited in Robin A. Parry, *Worshipping Trinity: Coming Back to the Heart of Worship* (Eugene, OR: Cascade Books, 2013), 131.

32. Thomas, *They Like to Never*, 117–22.

33. W. E. B. DuBois observed at the turn of the twentieth century that the three things that characterized the religion of the slave were the preacher, the music, and the frenzy (*The Souls of Black Folk* [Chicago: A. C. McClurg Publishers, 1903], 116). See also Donald G. Mathews, *Religion in the Old South* (Chicago: University of Chicago Press, 1977), 185–236; Eugene D. Genovese, *Roll Jordan Roll: The World Slaves Made Together* (New York: Vintage Books, 1972), 255–84; and Walter F. Pitts Jr., *Old Ship of Zion: The Afro-Baptist Ritual in the African Diaspora* (New York: Oxford University Press, 1993), 59–90.

34. Thomas, *They Like to Never*, 23.

35. William C. Turner is in agreement with Mitchell and Thomas when he asserts that to decouple emotion and reasoned reflection from black preaching unravels and erodes the very nexus from which the power of black preaching emerges. See Jana Childers and Clayton J. Schmidt, eds., *Performance in Preaching: Bringing the Sermon to Life* (Grand Rapids: Baker Academic, 2008), 86.

36. Josef Pieper, *In Tune with the World: A Theory of Festivity* (South Bend, IN: St. Augustine's Press, 1999), 86.

37. Geoffrey Wainwright, *Doxology: The Praise of God in Worship, Doctrine, and Life* (New York: Oxford University Press, 1980), 107–8; see also Powery, *Spirit Speech*, 31.

38. William Shakespeare, *The Tragedy of Macbeth* (New York: Simon and Schuster Inc., 1959), 86.

39. Moeller, *Calvin's Doxology*, 57.

Chapter 4. Festivity Theory and the Origins of Celebration.

1. Henry Mitchell, *Celebration and Experience in Preaching* (Nashville: Abingdon Press, 1990), 139. This is the first time Mitchell uses the term "joyous praise" to define *celebration*. Mitchell's definition of celebration as "purposefully focused emotional expression," comes in the 2008 revised edition, 35.

2. Frank A. Thomas, *They Like to Never Quit Praisin' God*, rev. ed. (Cleveland: Pilgrim Press, 2013), 49.

3. Ibid., 108.

4. I say for the "most part" because Mitchell rightly defines *celebration* in one instance as "joyous praise."

5. Mitchell quotes "educational research," not theology, as the major underpinning for his thoughts on the functionality of celebration: "Educational research has confirmed the idea that what we celebrate (get emotional about) we retain far longer. Educators have joined the healers in affirming that celebration provides what I have mentioned as the 'ecstatic reinforcement' of the lesson or content offered in the sermon." See Mitchell, *Celebration*, 30.

6. Josef Pieper argues that only religious rituals and celebrations could be called festivals. See Josef Pieper, *In Tune with the World: A Theory of Festivity* (South Bend, IN: St. Augustine's Press, 1999), 35–36. For a definition of *ritual*, see Anthony T. Padovano, *Presence and Structure: A Reflection on Celebration, Worship, and Faith* (New York: Paulist Press, 1976), 19.

7. Victor Turner, ed., *Celebration: Studies in Festivity and Ritual* (Washington, DC: Smithsonian Institution Press, 1982), 201.

8. *American Heritage Dictionary*, 4th edition (2000); *The New Oxford American Dictionary* (New York: Oxford University Press, 2005), 274.

9. Russell Shaw, ed., "Celebration, Liturgical," in *Our Sunday Visitor's Encyclopedia of Catholic Doctrine* (Huntington, IN: Our Sunday Visitor Publishing, 1998), 85–87. The word *celebration* is derived from the Latin *celeber*, which means "numerous, much frequented" and is related to the vivacity generated by a crowd of people with shared purposes and common values. The linguistic roots of the word group *celebration / to celebrate / celebrated* have to do with a large number or a multitude: a great assembly that comes together to salute the glory or the achievements of important events or personages. *Celebration* can also mean a concourse or a numerous assemblage of persons to keep a feast or a festival, while *to celebrate* is to go in great numbers to the solemnization of a feast, where the praises of a person or a thing are "celebrated," that is, made known by extolling them.

10. Pieper, *In Tune*, 35.

11. Harvey Cox, *Feast of Fools*, 16–17.

12. Ibid., 22. Cox draws on the works of Roger Caillois, who believes that festivity is mainly marked by a resurgence of excess and chaos, and he borrows from Josef Pieper's work *In Tune with the World* (Ibid., 22–23).

13. Ibid., 10–11.

14. Leon F. Litwack, *Been in the Storm so Long: The Aftermath of Slavery* (New York: Vintage Books, 1979), 107.

15. Cox, *Feast of Fools*, 24–26.

16. While Cox draws heavily on Pieper's *In Tune with the World*, he also notes the importance of writers on the order of Gerardus van der Leeuw and John Huizinga in *Homo Ludens* and their understandings of festivity as a form of play. See Ibid., 182, footnotes. Drawing in part on the works of Pieper, Roger Caillois, Hugo Rahner, and other festivity theorists, Cox further narrows the essentials of festivity, explains them in contemporary language, and reframes them into three essential characteristics, all of which can be found in black culture and religion.

17. Ibid., 22.

18. Ibid., 23.

19. Litwack, *Been in the Storm*, 116, notes that freed slaves would often celebrate by dressing themselves in their masters' and mistresses' finest clothes after their former owners' hasty departure.

20. Ralph C. Wood, *Contending for the Faith: The Church's Engagement with Culture* (Waco, TX: Baylor University Press, 2003), 172.

21. Ibid.

22. Ibid., Wood claims that blacks are making a theological statement about worship in the way they dress on Sunday mornings.

23. Cox, *Feast of Fools*, 23.

24. Ibid., 24. This festivity of which Cox speaks is often on vivid display in Princeton, New Jersey, when Princeton University alums return to campus during reunion week festivities.

25. Pieper, *In Tune*, 19–20.

26. Cox, *Feast of Fools*, 13.

27. Pieper, *In Tune*, 19.

28. Cox, *Feast of Fools*, 23.

29. Laurence Bergreen, *Louis Armstrong: An Extravagant Life* (New York: Broadway Books, 1997), 31–32.

30. Ibid.

31. Cox, *Feast of Fools*, 49.

32. Ibid., 23.

33. Ibid.

34. Wyatt T. Walker, *Millennium Papers: The Walker File '98–'99* (New York: Martin Luther King Fellows Press, 2000), 55–71.

35. Cox, *Feast of Fools*, 24.

36. Ibid., 7.

37. Ibid., 22–23.

38. Pieper, *In Tune*, 3–4.
39. Cox, *Feast of Fools*, 26.
40. Bergreen, *Louis Armstrong*, 32.
41. Pieper, *In Tune*, 17.
42. D. A. Carson, ed., *Worship: Adoration and Action* (Eugene, OR: Wipf & Stock, 1984), 203.
43. Pieper, *In Tune*, 15.
44. Ibid., 16–17.
45. Ibid., 17.
46. Ibid., 22.
47. Ibid.
48. Ibid., 23.
49. Ibid.
50. Donald Getz, "The Nature and Scope of Festival Studies," *International Journal of Event Management Research* 5 (2010): 1–47.
51. Alessandro Falissi, "Festival: Definition and Morphology," in *Time out of Time: Essays on the Festival*, ed. A. Falassi (Albuquerque: University of New Mexico Press, 1987), 2. Falassi goes on to list additional meanings of festival as (b) the annual celebration of a notable person or event, or the harvest of an important product; (c) a cultural event consisting of a series of performances of works in the fine arts, often devoted to a single artist or genre; (d) a fair; (e) generic gaiety, conviviality, cheerfulness (Ibid., 2–3).
52. Roger Caillois, *Man and the Sacred* (Urbana: University of Illinois Press, 1959), 99.
53. Pieper, *In Tune*, 35.
54. Ibid., 36–37. Pieper claims that this definition—the festival as holy time—continues to be the essential trait of festivity and is present in the midst of society today in the form of the praise given in the rituals of worship.
55. Ibid., 31. This affirmation of which Pieper speaks is not only of God but also of the world.
56. Ibid., 31, 38.
57. Richard Lischer, *A Theology of Preaching: The Dynamics of the Gospel* (Eugene, OR: Wipf & Stock, 1992), 13. For other forms of praise—word-centered, sacramental, spontaneous, and silent—see Daniel W. Hardy and David F. Ford's *Jubilate: Theology in Praise* (London: Darton, Longman, & Todd, 1984), 13–23.
58. Geoffrey Wainwright, *Doxology: The Praise of God in Worship, Doctrine, and Life* (New York: Oxford University Press, 1980), 45.
59. Mitchell, *Celebration*, 26.
60. Thomas, *They Like to Never*, 108.
61. Ibid., 30.
62. Ibid., 45.

63. Mitchell, *Celebration*, 30, 63.
64. Wainwright, "The Praise of God," 39.
65. Mitchell, *Celebration*, 30.
66. Ruth C. Duck, *Worship for the Whole People of God: Vital Worship for the 21st Century* (Louisville, KY: Westminster John Knox Press, 2013), 41.
67. Miroslav Volf, "Reflections on a Christian Way of Being-in-the-World," in Carson, *Worship*, 207–8.
68. Ibid.
69. Ibid., 211.
70. Luke Powery, *Spirit Speech: Lament and Celebration in Preaching* (Nashville: Abingdon Press, 2009), 134.

Chapter 5: A Theology of Praise in Its Multiple Expressions

1. Timothy A. Lenchak, "Praise," in *The Collegeville Pastoral Dictionary of Biblical Theology*, ed. Carroll Stuhlmueller (Collegeville, MN: Liturgical Press, 1996), 752.
2. Ibid.; see also Clayton J. Schmit, *Too Deep for Words: A Theology of Liturgical Expression* (Louisville, KY: Westminster John Knox Press, 2002), 43–59.
3. Lenchak, "Praise," 752.
4. Ralph P. Martin, *The Worship of God: Some Theological, Pastoral, and Practical Reflection* (Grand Rapids: Wm. B. Eerdmans Publishing Co., 1982), 20.
5. Ibid., 21.
6. Ibid.
7. Robert F. Youngblood, "Praise," *Nelson's New Illustrated Bible Dictionary* (New York: Thomas Nelson, 1995), 1022.
8. Frank C. Senn, "The Challenge of Pentecostal Praise and Orthodox Theology," *Lutheran Forum* 39, no. 3 (Fall 2005): 22.
9. Ibid.
10. Gerhard, Kittel, ed., *Theological Dictionary of the New Testament* (Grand Rapids: Wm. B. Eerdmans Publishing Co., 1964), 1:177.
11. Martin, *Worship*, 23.
12. Ibid., 23–24.
13. John M. Quinn, *Praise in St. Augustine: Readings and Reflections* (Norwell, MA: Christopher Publishing House, 1987), 1–3.
14. Ibid., vii.
15. Pieper, *In Tune*, 38.
16. Martin, *Worship*, 27–28.
17. Ibid., 28.
18. David F. Ford and Daniel W. Hardy, eds., *Living in Praise: Worshipping and Knowing God* (London: Darton, Longman, & Todd Ltd., 2005), 17–28.
19. Ibid., 23.

20. This mode has always been present in Christianity. Often it has been confined to private prayer, and frequently it has flowered afresh in movements of revival and renewal. It has been present in some form at the origins of many denominations. The past century has seen it spread in unprecedented ways, especially among Pentecostal churches and charismatic movements. "What is offered is not an alternative to word and sacrament but a new life and power to both of these, with an atmosphere which actualizes the 'logic of over-flow' in various ways: in the expectation that God will act and speak, in the freedom to express adoration in a wide range of bodily as well as verbal behavior, in the physical contact between worshipers (kiss of peace, handshake, holding hands, laying-on-of-hands), and in the exercise of various gifts" (ibid., 24–25).

21. Ibid., 26–27.

22. Herbert Bateman, ed., *Authentic Worship: Hearing Scripture's Voice, Applying its Truths* (Grand Rapids: Kregel Publications, 2002), 283.

23. Eric Werner, "The Doxology in Synagogue and Church: A Liturgico-Musical Study," *Hebrew Union College Annual* 19 (1945–46): 277.

24. Ibid., 278.

25. A statement ascribing something, especially to the deity.

26. Geoffrey Wainwright, "The Praise of God in the Theological Reflection of the Church," *Interpretation* 39 (1985): 38.

27. Donald Coggan, *The Sacrament of the Word* (Great Britain: Fount Paperbacks, 1987), 112.

28. Henry Mitchell, *Celebration and Experience in Preaching* (Nashville: Abingdon Press, 2008), 27.

29. H. Yavin, "Modern 'Doxologies' in Biblical Research," in *Judaic Perspectives on Ancient Israel*, ed. Jacob Neusner, Baruch A. Levine, and Ernest S. Frerichs (Philadelphia: Fortress Press, 1987), 271–80.

30. Ibid., 271. Yavin adds that hymns and liturgies are not the only place where doxological endings are found. There is a long tradition in the ancient Near East of nonliturgical, "literary" doxologies, doxologies at the conclusion of literary compositions. Sometimes the name in the doxology is a main character or one who has played a major role in the composition, as in "praise to holy Lugalbanda" (*ku-lugal-ban-da za-mi*) in the Sumerian Lugalbanda epic. In other cases the doxology appears to be more pro forma. Thus Sumerian compositions of diverse genres—epics, disputations, proverb collections—end with praise to a deity. The deity is often, but not always, Nisaba, the goddess of writing.

31. Ibid., 271.

32. Ibid., 272.

33. Ibid., 272–73.

34. Ibid., 274.

35. Cleophus LaRue, "The Necessity of the Wilderness" (unpublished sermon, Princeton Theological Seminary, Princeton NJ, June 16, 2014); see entire sermon in the appendix.

36. Gardner C. Taylor, unpublished sermon, Concord Baptist Church, Brooklyn, NY, spring 1988. This particular oral formulation is known as a run in black preaching and is often used by black preachers when they close out a sermon that focuses on Jesus Christ. Its origin is unknown; it is simply one of the public treasures one finds in black preaching.

37. See unpublished sermon "Why Bother?" in the appendix.

38. Yavin, "Modern 'Doxologies,'" 275.

39. Claudette Anderson Copeland, "Tamar's Torn Robe," in Cleophus J. LaRue, ed., *This Is My Story: Testimonies and Sermons of Black Women in Ministry* (Louisville, KY: Westminster John Knox Press, 2005), 113–18. See entire sermon reprinted in the appendix.

40. Yavin, "Modern 'Doxologies,'" 276.

41. Cleophus J. LaRue, "It Will Surely Come," *The Princeton Seminary Bulletin* (July 1999).

42. Yavin, "Modern 'Doxologies,'" 273.

43. See entire sermon printed in the appendix.

44. Yavin, "Modern 'Doxologies,'" 278.

45. Brian K. Blount, "Rise!" in *Invasion of the Dead: Preaching Resurrection* (Louisville, KY: Westminster John Knox Press, 2014), 109–20. See entire sermon reprinted in the appendix.

46. Ibid., 119–20.

47. Yavin, "Modern 'Doxologies,'" 276.

48. Ibid., 278.

Conclusion

1. Henry Mitchell, *Celebration and Experience in Preaching* (Nashville: Abingdon Press, 1990), 62–63.

2. Frank A. Thomas, *They Like to Never Quit Praisin' God*, rev. ed. (Cleveland: Pilgrim Press, 2013), 108.

3. Ibid.

4. Mitchell, *Celebration*, 30.

5. Ruth C. Duck, *Worship for the Whole People of God: Vital Worship for the 21st Century* (Louisville, KY: Westminster John Knox Press, 2013), 41.

6. D. A. Carson, ed., *Worship: Adoration and Action* (Eugene, OR: Wipf & Stock, 1984), 211.

7. Josef Pieper, *In Tune with the World: A Theory of Festivity* (South Bend, IN: St. Augustine's Press, 1999), 36–37. Festivals were regarded as "holy time," a time in which people affirmed God and God's creation.

8. Carson, *Worship*, 211.
9. Ibid., 154.
10. Ibid., 156.

Appendix: Sermons

1. An unpublished sermon first preached by Cleophus LaRue at Princeton Theological Seminary, Princeton, NJ, June 16, 2014.
2. An unpublished sermon first preached by Cleophus LaRue at Fifth Avenue Presbyterian Church, New York, December 7, 2008.
3. The late Dr. P. S. Wilkinson Sr. was the pastor of the New Light Baptist Church in San Antonio, Texas, for forty-six years and the president of the American Baptist State Convention of Texas. He preached this sermon at the Centennial Celebration of the American Baptist Western District Association in August, 1972, at the Mt. Salem Baptist Church in Victoria, Texas.
4. Brian K. Blount, "Rise!" in *Invasion of the Dead: Preaching Resurrection* (Louisville, KY: Westminster John Knox Press, 2014), 109–20.
5. Claudette Anderson Copeland, "Tamar's Torn Robe," in Cleophus J. LaRue, ed., *This Is My Story: Testimonies and Sermons of Black Women in Ministry* (Louisville, KY: Westminster John Knox Press, 2005), 113–18.
6. Cleophus J. LaRue, "It Will Surely Come," *The Princeton Seminary Bulletin* 20, no. 2 (July 1999): 189–92.
7. William Ernest Henley, "Invictus," Poetry Foundation, http://www.poetryfoundation.org/poem/182194.
8. T. S. Eliot, "Ash-Wednesday," in *Collected Poems 1909–1962* (New York: Harcourt Brace & Co., 1991), 83.

Bibliography

Alexander, Estrelda Y. *Black Fire Reader: A Documentary Resource on African American Pentecostalism.* Eugene, OR: Cascade Books, 2013.

Alexander, Michelle. *The New Jim Crow: Mass Incarceration in the Age of Colorblindness.* New York: The New Press, 2012.

Allen, O. Wesley, ed. *The Renewed Homiletic.* Minneapolis: Fortress Press, 2010.

Augustine. *On Christian Doctrine.* Reprint, translated by D. W. Robertson Jr., New York: Macmillan, 1987.

Bartow, Charles L. *God's Human Speech: A Practical Theology of Proclamation.* Grand Rapids: Wm. B. Eerdmans Publishing Co., 1997.

Bateman, Herbert W. *Authentic Worship: Hearing Scripture's Voice, Applying Its Truths.* Grand Rapids: Kregel Publications, 2002.

Bergreen, Laurence. *Louis Armstrong: An Extravagant Life.* New York: Broadway Books, 1997.

Blount, Brian K. *Invasion of the Dead: Preaching Resurrection.* Louisville, KY: Westminster John Knox Press, 2014.

Bond, Adam. *The Imposing Preacher: Samuel DeWitt Proctor and Black Public Faith.* Minneapolis: Fortress Press, 2013.

Branch, Taylor. *Parting the Waters: America in the King Years 1954–63.* New York: Simon & Schuster, 1988.

Brown, Sally A., and Patrick D. Miller, eds. *Lament: Reclaiming Practices in Pulpit, Pew, and Public Square.* Louisville, KY: Westminster John Knox Press, 2005.

Caillois, Roger. *Man and the Sacred.* Urbana: University of Illinois Press, 2001.

Carson, D. A., ed. *Worship: Adoration and Action.* Eugene, OR: Wipf & Stock Publishers. 1993.

Childers, Jana, and Clayton J. Schmit, eds. *Performance in Preaching: Bringing the Sermon to Life.* Grand Rapids: Baker Academic, 2008.

Coggan, Donald. *The Sacrament of the Word.* Great Britain: Fount Paperbacks, 1987.

Collins, Mary. "Doxology, Yes: But Who is Our God? *Currents in Theology and Mission* 26, no. 4 (August 1999): 245–56.

Cox, Harvey. *The Feast of Fools: A Theological Essay on Festivity and Fantasy.* New York: Harper & Row, 1969.

Douthat, Ross. *Bad Religion: How We Became a Nation of Heretics.* New York: Free Press, 2012.

DuBois, W. E. B. *The Souls of Black Folk.* Chicago: A. C. McClurg Publishers, 1903.

Duck, Ruth C. *Worship for the Whole People of God.* Louisville, KY: Westminster John Knox Press, 2013.

Eslinger, Richard L. *A New Hearing: Living Options in Homiletic Method.* Nashville: Abingdon Press, 1987.

Falassi, Alessandro, ed. *Time Out of Time: Essays on the Festival.* Albuquerque: University of New Mexico Press, 1967.

Ford, David F., and Daniel W. Hardy, eds. *Living In Praise: Worshipping and Knowing God.* Grand Rapids: Baker Academic, 2005.

Genovese, Eugene D. *Roll Jordan Roll: The World Slaves Made Together.* New York: Vintage Press, 1972.

Hall, Douglas John. *Thinking the Faith: Christian Theology in a North American Context.* Minneapolis: Fortress Press, 1989.

Highfield, Ron. *Great Is the Lord: Theology for the Praise of God.* Grand Rapids: Wm. B. Eerdmans Publishing Co., 2008.

Holmes, Barbara A. *Joy Unspeakable: Contemplative Practices of the Black Church.* Minneapolis: Fortress Press, 2004.

LaRue, Cleophus J., ed. *This Is My Story: Testimonies and Sermons of Black Women in Ministry.* Louisville, KY: Westminster John Knox Press, 2005.

Lenchak, Timothy A. "Praise." In *The Collegeville Dictionary of Biblical Theology.* Collegeville, MN: Liturgical Press, 1996.

Lischer, Richard. *A Theology of Preaching: The Dynamics of the Gospel.* Eugene, OR: Wipf & Stock, 1992.

Litwack, Leon F. *Been in the Storm So Long: The Aftermath of Slavery.* New York: Vintage Books, 1979.

Manning, Frank E. *The Celebration of Society: Perspectives on Contemporary Cultural Performance.* Bowling Green, OH: Bowling Green University Popular Press, 1983.

Martin, Ralph P. *The Worship of God: Some Theological, Pastoral, and Practical Reflection.* Grand Rapids: Wm. B. Eerdmans Publishing Co., 1982.

Massey, James Earl. *The Responsible Pulpit.* Anderson, IN: Warren Press, 1974.

Mathews, Donald G. *Religion in the Old South.* Chicago: University of Chicago Press, 1977.

Maynard-Reid, Pedrito U. *Diverse Worship: African-American, Caribbean and Hispanic Perspectives.* Downers Grove, IL: InterVarsity Press, 2000.

McMickle, Marvin. "Effectiveness in Preaching: A Study of the Preferences in Sermons and the Influence of Sermons upon a Black Congregation." DMin project. Princeton, NJ: Princeton Theological Seminary, 1983.

Mitchell, Henry H. *Black Preaching.* San Francisco: Harper & Row, 1970.

———. *The Recovery of Preaching.* San Francisco: Harper & Row, 1977.

———. *Celebration and Experience in Preaching.* Nashville: Abingdon Press, 1990.

———. *Celebration and Experience in Preaching*, rev. ed. Nashville: Abingdon Press, 2008.

Moeller, Pamela Ann. *Calvin's Doxology: Worship in the 1559* Institutes *with a View to Contemporary Renewal*. Allison Park: Pickwick Publications, 1997.

Moss III, Otis. *Blue Note Preaching in a Post-Soul World: Finding Hope in an Age of Despair*. Louisville, KY: Westminster John Knox Press, 2015.

Old, Hughes Oliphant. *Themes and Variations for a Christian Doxology*. Grand Rapids: Wm. B. Eerdmans Publishing Co., 1992.

———. *Worship: Reformed According to Scripture*. Revised. Louisville, KY: Westminster John Knox Press, 2002.

Padovano, Anthony T. *Presence and Structure: A Reflection on Celebration, Worship, and Faith*. New York: Paulist Press, 1976.

Parry, Robin A. *Worshipping Trinity: Coming Back to the Heart of Worship*. Eugene, OR: Cascade Books, 2012.

Pieper, Josef. *In Tune with the World: A Theory of Festivity*. South Bend, IN: St. Augustine's Press, 1999.

Pitt-Watson, Ian. *Preaching: A Kind of Folly*. Philadelphia: Westminster Press, 1976.

Pitts, Walter F. *Old Ship of Zion: The Afro-Baptist Ritual in the African Diaspora*. New York: Oxford University Press, 1993.

Powery, Luke A. *Spirit Speech: Lament and Celebration in Preaching*. Nashville: Abingdon Press, 2009.

Quinn, John M. *Praise in St. Augustine: Readings and Reflections*. Norwell, MA: Christopher Publishing House, 1987.

Raboteau, Albert. *A Fire in the Bones: Reflections on African American Religious History*. Boston: Beacon Press, 1995.

Rayburn, Robert Gibson. "Worship in the Reformed Tradition." *The Presbyterian* 6, no. 1 (Spring 1980): 17–32.

Rice, Charles L. *The Embodied Word: Preaching as Art and Liturgy*. Minneapolis: Fortress Press, 1991.

Saliers, Don. *Worship as Theology: A Foretaste of Glory Divine*. Nashville: Abingdon Press, 1994.

Schmemann, Alexander. *Introduction to Liturgical Theology*. Portland, OR: American Orthodox Press, 1966.

Schmit, Clayton J. *Too Deep for Words: A Theology of Liturgical Expression*. Louisville, KY: Westminster John Knox Press, 2002.

Scouteris, Constantine. "Doxology, the Language of Orthodoxy." *Greek Orthodox Theological Review* 38, no. 1–4 (Spring–Winter 1993): 153–62.

Segler, Frank M. *Christian Worship: Its Theology and Practice*. Nashville: Broadman Press, 1967.

Senn, Frank C. "The Challenge of Pentecostal Praise and Orthodox Theology." *Lutheran Forum* 39, no. 3 (Fall 2005): 16–24.

Smith, Robert Jr. *Doctrine that Dances: Bringing Doctrinal Preaching and Teaching to Life*. Nashville: B&H Publishing Group, 2008.

Thomas, Frank A. *They Like to Never Quit Praisin' God*. Cleveland: United Church Press, 1997; rev. ed., Cleveland: Pilgrim Press, 2013.

Turner, Victor, ed. *Celebration: Studies in Festivity and Ritual*. Washington, D. C.: Smithsonian Institute Press, 1982.

Wainwright, Geoffrey. *Doxology: The Praise of God in Worship, Doctrine, and Life*. New York: Oxford University Press, 1980.

———. "The Praise of God in the Theological Reflection of the Church." *Interpretation* 9, no. 1 (Jan 1985): 34–45.

Walker, Wyatt Tee. *The Soul of Black Worship: A Trilogy*. New York: Martin Luther King Fellows Press, 1984.

———. *Millennium Papers: The Walker File '98; '99*. New York: Martin Luther King Fellows Press, 2000.

Webber, Robert E. *Worship Is a Verb*. Nashville: Abbot Martyn, 1992.

Welker, Michael, and Cynthia A. Jarvis, eds. *Loving God with Our Minds: The Pastor as Theologian*. Grand Rapids: Wm. B. Eerdmans Publishing Co., 2004.

Werner, Eric. "The Doxology in Synagogue and Church: A Liturgico-Musical Study, *Hebrew Union College Annual* 19 (1945–1946): 275–351.

Wood, Ralph C. *Contending for the Faith: The Church's Engagement with Culture*. Waco, TX: Baylor University Press, 2003.

Woodruff, William J. "Celebration," in *Baker's Evangelical Dictionary of Biblical Theology*. Edited by Walter A. Elwell. Grand Rapids: Baker Books.

Yavin, H. " 'Modern 'Doxologies' in Biblical Research." in *Judaic Perspectives on Ancient Israel*. Edited by Jacob Neusner, Baruch A. Levine, and Ernest S. Frerichs. Philadelphia: Fortress Press, 1987.

CPSIA information can be obtained
at www.ICGtesting.com
Printed in the USA
LVOW04s0034070117
520028LV00013B/293/P